Thomas Paine's
The Age of Reason
Part Three

by
Robert Shear

ISBN:0692234764
ISBN-13:978-0692234761

Age of Reason Publishing
646 South Main Street
Suite 222
Cedar City, Utah
84720

TheAgeofReason.us

DEDICATION

To Laura and Colin – A marriage made in Nature

CONTENTS

Introduction:
Thomas Paine and the Age of Reason   i

Acknowledgments   vi

Preface to Part Three   ix

Preface to Part Two   xi

I   Religion, Rights and the Advance of Science   1

II   The End of Deism   11

III   The Scriptures Revisited   23

IV   The New Religions   37

V   The Immorality of Religious Indoctrination   55

VI   Church and State in the New Millennium   65

VII   Conclusions   79

About the Author   83

Notes   85

INTRODUCTION:
Thomas Paine and The Age of Reason

Thomas Paine was born in Thetford, England in 1737, where his mother belonged to the Church of England, in which he was confirmed, and his father to the Society of Friends (the Quakers). As a child he found religious lessons about the crucifixion of Jesus distressing, and devoid of inspiring message. Rather, from a young age he found the teachings of the churches to be works of disturbed imagination, their institutional advocates seemingly more self-interested than Christ-like. At the age of 56, he summarized a lifetime of thought on the subject of religion in his opening chapter of *The Age of Reason* (Part One):

> I believe in one God, and no more; and I hope for happiness beyond this life.

> I believe the equality of man, and I believe that religious duties consist of doing justice, loving mercy, and endeavoring to make our fellow-creatures happy...

> I do not believe in the creed professed by the Jewish Church, by the Roman Church, by the Greek Church, by the Turkish Church by the Protestant Church, nor by any church that I know of. My own mind is my own church.

> All national institutions of churches, whether Jewish, Christian or Turkish, appear to me no other than human inventions set up to terrify and enslave mankind, and monopolize power and profit.

These words are still shocking to even the most committed of religious critics in the 21st century. The more so they were written by one of America's most visionary Founders - by the man who more than any other inspired his countrymen to accept that separation from England was inevitable, that the time for Revolution was upon them. His first published pamphlet, *Common Sense,* laid out in straightforward language the case for Independence and against the legitimacy of hereditary monarchy.

Believed the first to have written the words *The United States of America*, Paine was no sunshine patriot. He shouldered his musket and joined the Continental Army. His series of pamphlets on *The Crisis*, the first literally written on the night of battle, so bolstered spirits that General Washington ordered them read to the troops. The opening words of that series: *"These are the times that try men's souls"* became a battle cry of the American Revolution inspiring the outnumbered Patriots to victory over superior British forces. In 1783 he wrote the last of their number, beginning "The times that tried men's souls are over." He published all of these works anonymously, and from their sale he received no royalties, instead gifting them to the nation.

Paine's battles, however, were far from over. The revolutionary attack on Monarchy sent chills throughout Europe. Jefferson was made Minister to France, succeeding Benjamin Franklin, who had done his part to spread revolutionary spirit by publishing in Paris some of America's State Constitutions. There to interest French experts in his design for an iron bridge, in 1787 Paine continued his friendship with Jefferson, and with their comrade in arms the Marquis de Lafayette, who had returned from his role in the American Revolution nothing short of a rock star. It was Lafayette who ultimately ordered the demolition of the Bastille, entrusting to Paine its main key for delivery as a gift to then-President Washington.

When the French Revolution came under attack by the English Parliamentarian Edmund Burke, it was Thomas Paine, then in England, whose spirited defense - *Rights of Man* - was most widely embraced, and condemned. His new manifesto labeled a seditious work, Paine came under attack in England and again departed for France to a hero's welcome. There he was one of two foreigners seated in the National Convention established to write a democratic charter for that country.

Under political and military pressure from royalists across Europe, the Revolution faltered, its leaders turning against one another. Paine's plea to spare Louis XVI - whose support for the American Revolution he had helped to obtain - nearly cost him his own life. As the author explains in the Preface to Part Two, his situation in Paris became difficult, and then untenable. Fearing his own end was near, and that France was descending into chaos, he resolved to prepare what he had planned to be his final work, which he titled *The Age of Reason*. In this document he sought to dismantle the foundation of *revealed religion*, and to offer in its stead a simple moral code based on his belief in a benevolent God who revealed himself not in dreams, visions or holy books, but in the intricate designs of Nature.

Completed as he awaited the policeman's knock, the first Part of *The Age of Reason* was printed in January 1794 while Paine was imprisoned in Paris anticipating execution. Paine's friends sought to claim him as an American citizen and secure his release, but were not supported by Jefferson's replacement as Minister to France, Governeur Morris. Paine's direct plea for assistance was ignored by President Washington.

Spared the guillotine by an apparent fluke, it was nearly two years later that Paine published Part Two, written while he recovered from a nearly fatal prison illness in the home of the new American Minister, future President James Monroe. The book was attacked from all sides, its author labeled Infidel. At the same time *The Age of Reason*'s defense of Deism was extensively plagiarized by others and even used in argument against Paine, as a challenge to his own supposed atheism.

Having been left to his fate by Morris, and abandoned by his former supporter Washington, Paine was understandably bitter. He finally returned to America in 1802 on a warship sent by President Jefferson, such was the continuing threat he faced from British royalists for his calls for revolution in England and its invasion by France.

On his return to America, Paine was welcomed by Jefferson as a guest, and advised to withhold further attacks on Religion. Many old friends had abandoned him, both those who had always understood his religious beliefs as well as those who found them shocking. His last printed piece[1], which some have represented as the original Part Three of this work, found no publisher and only a small run was produced at the author's own expense.

Thomas Paine died in 1809 with none of the honors commensurate with the many ways in which his career has helped to shape our modern world. Six persons were in attendance at his burial, the story of which is sad enough to bring tears to a contemporary admirer.

After his death, Paine's long-time friend and heir Margaret Brazier Bonneville circulated a redacted version of his essay on the *Origins of Free-Masonry*, thought to be a portion of the original Part Three manuscript, which had been left to her in Paine's will.[2] The piece was quickly recognized as inauthentic in its apparent effort to rehabilitate the author's reputation among the religious, and therefor drew little attention. Some years later she was reported to be editing Paine's unpublished autobiography and collected works, which he had also left to her care. She, like Paine, never completed the task. After being placed in storage by her son, the original manuscript for Part Three of *The Age of Reason* was lost in a fire, along with the rest of his papers.[3]

EDITOR'S NOTE:

Though strident in its attack on the Bible, and on revealed religion in general, the ideas expressed in *The Age of Reason* were otherwise typical of an 18th century Deist. More engineer than scientist, Paine did not travel in the same intellectual circles as Franklin or Jefferson. As a result, when he published the first Parts of *The Age of Reason* it appears he was entirely unfamiliar with what by that time had been discovered of geology and the origins of life on Earth. He had no conception of "deep" time, as it is understood in geological terms. He was unaware of the evidence that then existed for the ascent of man through evolution. He died over a century before Einstein published his theory of special relativity, before the expansion of the Universe was understood or the Big Bang theorized. Were he to have possessed the knowledge now common among school children in the developed world, *The Age of Reason* would certainly have presented a much different view of the universe, and its author would undoubtedly have held yet more enlightened views.

The decision to prepare a new Part Three, to be written as Paine and casting myself as Editor, grew out of discussions held by a group of religious free-thinkers to which I belong. It was my task to introduce *The Age of Reason* by attempting to place the work in its historical context. When I finished, among the questions I posed to the group was what Thomas Paine would think now, if he knew what we know. What exactly would his current views be, given knowledge of what has transpired in the 220 years since *The Age of Reason* was first published? The following (apart from the Preface to Part Two, which is Paine's original) represents my attempt to answer those questions.

The reader may find this Part more interesting if familiar with Paine's original, though like all sequels it is meant to stand on its own and to be enjoyed by the first-time reader. The text refers frequently to Paine's earlier published thoughts and positions, which are reported faithfully here. The projections of where these thoughts would take him two centuries later are, I think, consistent with a fair judgment of the man and his character. If others disagree with my projections, I hope to hear from them. What could be better than to have one's work stimulate more interest and discussion regarding one of our country's great, and perhaps most under-appreciated founders?

It is my hope this project will be of interest to Thomas Paine's current admirers and may also help to bring new audiences to his prior works, along with a more just appreciation of his service to America and the world. In preparing his (very) long awaited new work for publication, I have attempted to present Mr. Paine's updated views in a familiar style, while contributing a sometimes more modern vocabulary. To those acquainted with the previous Parts of this work, or with the author's other writings, I trust the voice will be familiar. To the extent any element of this Part fails to ring true, or retains unnoticed errors, the fault is most definitely to be laid to the editor, and not to Mr. Paine.

R.S.

ACKNOWLEDGMENTS

I AM much indebted to Moncure Daniel Conway for his excellent biography and his compilation of my previous works published at the centenary of *The Age of Reason*. I have found his review of my writings and their impact most thoughtful, and for the most part consistent with my memory of events. I note but few errors in his reporting and conjecture,[4] and can, therefore, attest to greater accuracy in his work than in that of the Evangelists. As the products of my own effort to collect and edit my prior works and correspondence has been lost, I am grateful to have at hand Mr. Conway's able substitute.

In my efforts to determine the destiny of my final papers and other possessions, I have been aided by Gary Berton, Coordinator of the Institute for Thomas Paine Studies at Iona College in my adopted home town of New Rochelle. Mr. Berton also serves as Secretary of the Thomas Paine National Historical Association, which is based there. Thanks are due to the Association for their stewardship of what remains of these artifacts.

Somewhat less creditable, but at least worthy of a mention, is the work performed by the editor of this volume, to whom I owe thanks for calling to my attention the contributions of Mr. Conway and of several other authors. He has also introduced me to the many resources of the Internet through which I have located much useful information.

I am indebted to Rebecca Stott for her survey of a vast array of scientific information, much of it suppressed during my lifetime, and the excellent history of that suppression provided in her book *Darwin's Ghosts*. This book has also served as my introduction to the work of Charles Darwin, son of my English contemporary Erasmus Darwin, whose work was also unknown to me. An acquaintance of Franklin, but also unknown to me at the time was James Hutton, now regarded as the father of Geology, a science which has greatly progressed on account of his genius. I am indebted to John McPhee for my introduction to that science in his extraordinary book series *Annals of the Former World*.

My introduction to modern physics is derived first from the works of Stephen Hawking and Richard Feynman.

For my introduction to the enthusiastic religious movements centered in Upstate New York in the first half of the 19th century, I am indebted to Whitney Cross, and his excellent book *The Burned Over District*. I have found no better source for my review of the most enduring of those movements than in the works of the self-styled Mormon prophet, Joseph Smith. My understanding of the history of his religion has also been aided by the work of Mr. Cross, Juanita Brooks, Will Bagley and Jon Krakauer, and by the insights of my new friends Holly Bateman, Gordon Eddington and Peggy Strickling.

My understanding of the more personal aspects of what is called spirituality has been aided by William James' *Varieties of Religious Experience* and by Oliver Sacks' *Hallucinations*. My current editor has shared with me some interesting anecdotes connecting this type of experience with twentieth century religious enthusiasm and the Spiritualism found in the official biographies of the founders of Alcoholics Anonymous.

My understanding of the great reform movements which transformed America in the mid-nineteenth century (and again in the mid-twentieth) has been greatly aided by the writings of Frederick Douglass, Gerrit Smith, Jermain Wesley Loguen, Elizabeth Cady Stanton, Matilda Joslin Gage, Samuel J. May and Rep. John Lewis, along with those of contemporary scholars Sally Roesch Wagner and Milton Sernett.

I have enjoyed the pleasure of listening to several series of lectures made available through *The Great Courses.* These have helped to update me on what is now fundamental knowledge in physics, human psychology, and the early development of the Christian religion.[5] I have also enjoyed the perspectives provided on the latter subject by many authors, most recently that of Reza Aslan in his interesting portrayal of Jesus of Nazareth as *Zealot*.

My understanding of the continuing challenges to truth posed by modern churches has been informed by the work of evolutionary biologist Richard Dawkins and of the engineer and educator Bill Nye, among others. For his modern treat-ment of these issues, and of the natural origins of morality, I am indebted to Sam Harris, and his book *The Moral Land-scape.* A more fundamental understanding of Altruism has been acquired from the works of E.O. Wilson, particularly *The Social Conquest of Earth.* I am appreciative of the work of Mr. Christopher Hitchens, recently deceased, both for his brief treatise on *Rights of Man* and for his own work in the field of religion, most notably his book *God is Not Great.*

Among our national leaders, few compare in their defense of Human Rights or their guardianship of the First Amend-ment to President James E. Carter. His commitment to democ-racy and human rights brought these issues to the fore in the policies of our government during his Presidency and he has continued to labor in their service ever since. He and Mrs. Carter have traveled the world, studying, mediating and pro-posing creative solutions to key problems at home and abroad. I am especially impressed by his boldness, as a devout Chris-tian, in the defense of the separation of Church and State to be found in his prescient (2004) book *Our Endangered Values,* and his continuing efforts to separate religion from the oppres-sion of women in his very recent *A Call to Action.* Even greater praise is due his practical proposals for ending the immense suffering daily endured by the people of Palestine in his 2005 book *Palestine: Peace Not Apartheid.*

Finally, I wish to express my appreciation of all of the men and women who have labored over the past two centuries to advance the twin causes of Science and Human Rights. Through their efforts, often at the cost of their lives, they have elevated human dignity and freedom to new heights, and have pointed the way to a future where ignorance and superstition will no longer serve as the foundation of tyranny and exploitation of the many for the benefit of the few. It is to their memory this work is dedicated.

T.P.

PREFACE TO PART THREE

I AM long delayed in bringing before the public Part Three of *The Age of Reason*. There are several reasons for this, which need not be elaborated here. Having failed to see to the publication of my autobiography and annotated works as I had intended, I am saddened to note that all but fragments of that undertaking are lost, along with the original manuscript for Part Three of this work.

As the issues that concerned me two centuries ago are of lesser consequence now, it has been my decision to begin again, reviewing events in the interval and addressing the issues of the present day, rather than to attempt reconstruction of the former manuscript. The process by which this is achieved would be difficult to explain. I can attest there is nothing supernatural about it, but upon this point I have no more to offer.

Those familiar with the facts of my life following publication of *The Age of Reason*, will know my judgment in wishing it to be the last of my writings has been proved wise. Though at the time of our American Revolution my literary contributions (*Common Sense, American Crisis*) were widely regarded with esteem, and *Rights of Man* brought me some acclaim, the response to *The Age of Reason* was quite different, as I had expected it would be.

Where the agents of Monarchy were content to see me outlawed, the Churches spared no effort to see me destroyed. At the time of my death in 1809, I had been roundly denounced as an Atheist, rejected by the public, and left behind few mourners and fewer true friends. I emphasize this was to be expected, that I harbor no regrets for my actions and no ill will toward those who chose the comforts of ancient myth over the hazards of free thought. That was their right.

In the two centuries since I last put down this work, much has changed in the world. Indeed, more progress had already been made by 1795 - in the study of the earth, the heavens and of life on this planet - than ever I had dreamed. Of course, most knowledge of this progress remained suppressed by the churches whose foundations it so greatly threatened, and by the monarchs whose own tottering state was dependent on the legitimacy of their partners in tyranny. Thus, the unholy combination of Church and State continued to hold most of humanity in ignorance until well past the end of my days.

But no more! Our Age of Enlightenment did indeed lead to the liberation of science in combination with the advance of human rights, albeit through great struggle and to as yet only partial success. Witnessing the rapid growth in understanding of the natural world, the great political movements advancing ever forward the cause of Human Rights, and the violent reactions in what one hopes to be the death throes of religious superstition, I saw it was time to prepare for publication a new, and I trust, final Part of *The Age of Reason*.

It is my fond hope this volume will help to inspire my fellow citizens to finally free themselves from the tyranny and exploitation perpetuated by the teaching of supersticion, and to sweep away forever the last remnants of religious influence in their public affairs.

THOMAS PAINE

June, 2014

PREFACE TO PART TWO

I HAVE mentioned in the former part of the Age of Reason that it had long been my intention to publish my thoughts upon religion; but that I had originally reserved it to a later period in life intending it to be the last work I should undertake. The circumstances, however, which existed in France in the latter end of the year 1793, determined me to delay it no longer. The just and humane principles of the revolution, which philosophy had first diffused, had been departed from. The idea, always dangerous to society, as it is derogatory to the Almighty, that priests could forgive sins, though it seemed to exist no longer, had blunted the feelings of humanity, and prepared men for the commission of all manner of crimes. The intolerant spirit of Church persecutions had transferred itself into politics; the tribunal styled revolutionary, supplied the place of an inquisition; and the guillotine and the stake outdid the fire and fagot of the Church. I saw many of my most intimate friends destroyed, others daily carried to prison, and I had reason to believe, and had also intimations given me, that the same danger was approaching myself.

Under these disadvantages, I began the former part of the Age of Reason; I had, besides, neither Bible nor Testament[6] to refer to, though I was writing against both; nor could I procure any: notwithstanding which, I have produced a work that no Bible believer, though writing at his ease, and with a library of Church books about him, can refute.

Toward the latter end of December of that year, a motion was made and carried, to exclude foreigners from the Convention[7]. There were but two in it, Anacharsis Cloots and myself; and I saw I was particularly pointed at by Bourdon de l'Oise, in his speech on that motion.

Conceiving, after this, that I had but a few days of liberty, I sat down and brought the work to a close as speedily as possible; and I had not finished it more than six hours, in the state it has since appeared, before a guard came there, about three in the morning, with an order signed by the two Committees of public Safety and Surety General for putting me in arrestation as a foreigner, and conveyed me to the prison of the Luxembourg. I contrived, on my way there, to call on Joel Barlow, and I put the manuscript of the work into his hands: as more safe than in my possession in prison; and not knowing what might be the fate in France either of the writer or the work, I addressed it to the protection of the citizens of the United States.

It is with justice that I say that the guard who executed this order, and the interpreter of the Committee of General Surety who accompanied them to examine my papers, treated me not only with civility, but with respect. The keeper of the Luxembourg, Bennoit, a man of a good heart, showed to me every friendship in his power, as did also all his family, while he continued in that station. He was removed from it, put into arrestation, and carried before the tribunal upon a malignant accusation, but acquitted.

After I had been in the Luxembourg about three weeks, the Americans then in Paris went in a body to the Convention to reclaim me as their countryman and friend; but were answered by the President, Vadier, who was also President of the Committee of Surety-General, and had signed the order for my arrestation, that I was born in England. I heard no more, after this, from any person out of the walls of the prison till the fall of Robespierre, on the 9th of Thermidor — July 27, 1794.

About two months before this event I was seized with a fever, that in its progress had every symptom of becoming mortal, and from the effects of which I am not recovered. It was then that I remembered with renewed satisfaction, and congratulated myself most sincerely, on having written the former part of the Age of Reason. I had then but little expectation of surviving, and those about me had less. I know, therefore, by experience, the conscientious trial of my own principles.

I was then with three chamber comrades, Joseph Vanhuele, of Bruges; Charles Bastini, and Michael Rubyns, of Louvain. The unceasing and anxious attention of these three friends to me, by night and by day, I remember with gratitude and mention with pleasure. It happened that a physician (Dr. Graham) and a surgeon (Mr. Bond), part of the suite of General O'Hara, were then in the Luxembourg. I ask not myself whether it be convenient to them, as men under the English government, that I express to them my thanks, but should reproach myself if I did not; and also to the physician of the Luxembourg, Dr. Markoski.

I have some reason to believe, because I cannot discover any other cause, that this illness preserved me in existence. Among the papers of Robespierre that were examined and reported upon to the Convention by a Committee of Deputies, is a note in the hand-writing of Robespierre, in the following words:

"Demander que Thomas Paine soit decrete d'accusation, pour l'interet de l'Amerique autant que de la France"

(To demand that a decree of accusation be passed against Thomas Paine, for the interest of America, as well as of France).

From what cause it was that the intention was not put in execution I know not, and cannot inform myself, and therefore I ascribe it to impossibility, on account of that illness.[8]

The Convention, to repair as much as lay in their power the injustice I had sustained, invited me publicly and unanimously to return into the Convention, and which I accepted, to show I could bear an injury without permitting it to injure my principles or my disposition. It is not because right principles have been violated that they are to be abandoned.

I have seen, since I have been at liberty, several publications written, some in America and some in England, as answers to the former part of the Age of Reason. If the authors of these can amuse themselves by so doing, I shall not interrupt them. They may write against the work, and against me, as much as they please; they do me more service than they intend, and I can have no objection that they write on. They will find, however, by this second part, without its being written as an answer to them, that they must return to their work, and spin their cobweb over again. The first is brushed away by accident.

They will now find that I have furnished myself with a Bible and Testament; and I can say also that I have found them to be much worse books than I had conceived. If I have erred in anything in the former part of the Age of Reason, it has been by speaking better of some parts of those books than they have deserved.

I observe that all my opponents resort, more or less, to what they call Scripture evidence and Bible authority to help them out. They are so little masters of the subject, as to confound a dispute about authenticity with a dispute about doctrines; I will, however, put them right, that if they should be disposed to write any more, they may know how to begin.

THOMAS PAINE.

October, 1795

CHAPTER I

RELIGION, RIGHTS AND THE ADVANCE OF SCIENCE

I BEGAN Part One of *The Age of Reason* with a discussion of what I did, and did not believe at that time. I offered no criticism of those who believed otherwise, and have always stood fast in defense of all, without regard to their beliefs. In truth we do not choose our beliefs, and are as powerless to change them by an act of will as we are to change what we know of the natural world to some greater or lesser degree, simply by willing it. As we do not acquire knowledge of a subject simply by knowing it exists and wishing to know more of it, so we do not acquire or discharge beliefs simply because we think it might be better or more pleasant for us to have one or to lose another.

This being the case, on the subject of belief in general, and on religion in particular, we must approach our neighbor in a spirit of charity. We may also wish to consider when and how we lay new ideas before them or challenge their long held beliefs. But from the necessity of challenging ideas supported solely by superstition and tradition we must not shrink.

For beliefs to be altered requires an openness of mind, a willingness to question, access to new information, and the strength of character to examine one's own ideas in the light of others'. In their efforts to prevent adherents from falling away, churches have ever worked to prevent such free sharing of ideas and the exercise of free thought, curiosity, and independence of spirit.

The effects of these efforts, in concert with those of allied governments, have been to cultivate among their subjects a terror of authority and reluctance to examine the foundations of law or dogma, to suppress knowledge among the common people, and to promote weakness and submissiveness in the character of men and women. Little wonder many find it easier to go along with the demands of religious and civil authorities (or to pretend it) than to face the predictable consequences of daring to question, study, and apply their power of Reason to the important subject of religion.

Following my first profession of belief I pointed out the danger which comes from Mental Lying, i.e. from pretending to believe what one does not believe. Increasingly I see this danger reflected in the silence of men and women who know that much if not all of what they profess to believe on the subject of religion is not really true, who yet continue to support churches and allow their children to be indoctrinated with beliefs they no longer share.

Perhaps this is done out of a desire for fellowship in communities where the congregation is the primary social outlet, or for the opportunity to share with others in the quest for meaning and in the conduct of good works. Perhaps it is out of fear of losing social status or economic benefits, or of disappointing friends and relatives were they to speak plainly about their true beliefs or lingering doubts. For whatever reasons many continue to profess and to pass on to their children religions in which they do not fully believe, it is to this group I make a special appeal, as it is they who hold the key to a new Age of Enlightenment.

If all who know the truth about Religion will speak out plainly, will refuse any corruption of public policy by religious doctrine; will refuse to give deference to those who demand special privileges, convinced their own beliefs are sacred, above challenge, and morally superior to those of their neighbors; if all with doubts about the factual basis of their religion will but commit to their resolution through direct and unfettered inquiry, our country - and with it the world - will see a rebirth of Liberty, an explosion of understanding and a loosening of cruel restraint unmatched since Revolutionary times.

In the prior parts of this work I challenged Revealed Religion by showing the so-called sacred texts were in fact the work of human imagination, their mystical claims unsupported by evidence and contrary to reason. I proceed now to challenge on the same ground all supernatural beliefs, and their continued place of acceptance in a modern democratic society.

Progress in Human Rights

When the first Parts of this work were published, it was still too early to see to what extent our Revolution in America had brought lasting progress in advancing the rights of men and women, what we now call Human Rights. Our American Constitution was less than a decade old. The new Polish constitution was even younger, and distressingly short lived before that country was removed from the map of Europe by foreign kings. The Revolution in France had turned against itself, and hope for an England free of hereditary monarchy was as faint as it was fond.

Looking back from our current perspective, it is plain our American Revolution did indeed help to spark an unstoppable quest for liberty around the world. Albeit in fits and starts, America has continued to improve itself. France at last found stability, and progresses still as a nation without monarch or state religion. England alone, among the nations dearest to my heart, continues to live under the official rule - happily much weakened - of its usurper "royals" and an arrogant self-described aristocracy, still bowing to the (admittedly more enlightened) state church founded by Henry VIII.

While many of our eighteenth century dreams remain unrealized, progress has been nonetheless stunning. Throughout the world, Republican Democracy is the recognized standard of legitimate government. Nearly everywhere kings have been reduced to figureheads, and even in the most tyrannical of theocracies, at the very least the structures of popular self-rule are shown.

I do not wish to minimize the challenges which lie ahead. True Democracy is as much feared now as it was in the time of Jefferson. It is still common to see the stronger countries undermining democracy - sometimes fomenting revolutions and sponsoring coups - to serve their own political and commercial interests at the expense of weaker nations. Practical plans proposed centuries ago to improve the lot of the poorer classes have still not been adopted, and the gap between the common people and those hoarding massive amounts of undeserved and unneeded wealth is once again growing rapidly. Yet and still, what progress has been made!

Last year (2013) marked the 65th anniversary of the Universal Declaration of Human Rights, approved by the General Assembly of the United Nations without a dissenting vote. To behold this document - adopted by a global association of the world's nations - all but takes the breath away. Here stand the principles of Jefferson and Lafayette, accepted as the shared ideals of all nations.

It should be with great pride the American People reflect upon the role played by our country's representatives in bringing this Declaration before the world and seeing to its adoption. Equally we should be humbled to recall that while placing before the world a vision of equal rights for all, our country was still denying them by law and custom to a vast portion of its own people. Even at the present time, international treaties to secure the rights of Indigenous People, Children and the Disabled that have been signed by the United States all remain unratified.

Before us are the plans for a just world and a decent future for all of its inhabitants. Yet these ideals will not be achieved by wishing, as all past struggles for freedom attest. Their achievement will require further sacrifices, a fact we must face with boldness.

As we continue in our quest to extend equal rights to all, it is important we also reflect upon an important lesson, that being the extent to which past advances in Human Rights have led to new discoveries in Science, and how these, reciprocally, have advanced the cause of Human Rights.

Progress in Science

In Part One of this work, I addressed the System of the Universe as it was then known to me.[9] I could not have imagined at that time the discoveries yet to be made in astronomy and astrophysics, and how they would change our understanding of the universe and its origins. It was then commonly believed, as Newton had taught, the natural state of matter was *at rest*, and that its observed motion was testimony to the existence of a Divine Mover. More than a century would pass before this view was overthrown by the insights of Einstein, and the observations of LeMaitre and Hubble.[10]

While it could be clearly shown by reason alone the Genesis account of creation was fabulous, few in 1795 knew it was already possible to demonstrate this fact beyond a doubt. The world waited many decades to learn the true origin of species, revealed not in visions and holy books but through careful and systematic study of the natural world. In the decades following, our knowledge in all the sciences has continued to grow ever more rapidly, and as our technology has advanced, new realms of study have opened up. Among the most crucial of these to the present discussion are the sciences of the mind and of human behavior.

While much remains to be discovered, science has given us a fundamental understanding of the workings of the brain, and of the basic functions of perception, emotion, thought and belief. We can now see the origins of our impulse to seek patterns and to create myths, to form groups and to collaborate with one another as well as to separate our-selves into competing bands.

Inquiries into the workings of the brain have removed much of the mystery which once surrounded dreams, visions, voices in the mind and the natural disorders once mistaken for demonic possession. Perhaps most importantly, we now know the mind is wholly a function of the brain's interaction with our senses, and that all of our mental faculties, including memory, perception and self-awareness, reside entirely within the body and die with it. The existence of an immortal human spirit or soul – one which thinks, remembers or remains

5

interested in the affairs of the living - can no longer be seriously considered.

So thoroughly different is our understanding of the world and our role in it as to leave most of our 18th century beliefs in this realm blasted. The dismantling of old concepts has been more difficult for some than for others, and must be humbling to even the most secure and open minded. Lest the reader should imagine that I find no discomfort in the dis-solution of former beliefs, let me give assurance this is not the case.

I have previously written of the comfort I once took in the belief God watched over and protected His Creation. Pleasant as I still find this notion, its benefits come at too high a cost. If a mind wishes to be free, and to see clearly, it must let go of its fear of Nature in all her power and of the tricks of imagination used to hold fear at bay. It is, I believe, the duty of all to embrace this challenge with courage, for in so doing we free not only our own minds, but those of others, and open the door to possibilities as yet unimagined. I offer an example of this by observing the contributions unknowingly made to the cause of Science by the 18th century advocates for Human Rights:

It is only in retrospect that we have come to learn the motivations of one of my English countrymen in braving the charges of heresy and sedition to publish a Promethean work of science which has served as a foundation to our current understanding of Evolution (and which itself indirectly inspired a related work of still-popular literature[11]). I speak here of Erasmus Darwin, author of the groundbreaking (1795) work titled *Zoonomia*, in which he demonstrated the gradual progression of animal life from simple sea creatures to those ever more complex, showing this process of gradual change and adaptation over millions of years has led through to the evolution of modern humans.

Having previously published other important scientific works in the guise of romantic poetry,[12] Darwin found inspiration and courage in the progress of the American and French Revolutions, and in the trials[13] of those such as Priestly and myself, who facing mobs and prison ultimately had to flee

England for freer shores. Unwilling to withhold or disguise his observations any longer, Darwin proceeded to publish his findings despite the certainty of reprisal by Church and State.

There can be no doubt that his decision to publish - consequences be damned - not only directly advanced the cause of science in a most important way, but also provided the example needed by his son Charles to complete the writing of the greatest story ever told. Thus we see the intimate relationship, and reciprocal progress in the causes of science and human rights.

Churches Remain the Enemy of Both

There is no doubt Human Imagination has been the source of much progress, leading to many useful inventions, and inspiring great minds to derive important theories and principles from observations of nature. Human Imagination is also at the root of all fable and myth, and while this power opens vast fields of possibility for us to explore, it is the power of Reason which has shown us the way to separate wheat from chaff.

It is Human Reason which has taught us the methods of Science, and led to all the great discoveries which have in recent centuries trans-formed our world. There remains by contrast not a single useful invention, medical breakthrough, principle of mechanics, or feat of engineering which we can attribute to the discoveries of prophets, priests, shamans or other mystics. It is Science, elevated by Reason, which leads us to ever greater understanding of our world, and which has empowered humanity to achieve its dreams of prolonging life, conquering plagues, and travel to places once thought to be mere lights fixed in an imaginary dome covering a small flat world of recent creation. All useful discoveries illuminate this truth. By contrast, the dreams, visions and allegories of ancient people reveal no more truths about the universe than do the contemporary daydreams of children.

It may fairly be asked what matter if one's neighbor accepts as true the ancient myths, or ascribes his daily behavior to fluctuations in the strength of angels and demons? Should we deny to the suffering the comfort to be found in prayer, by denying that prayers are heard by God? Is hope for an afterlife - for reunification with lost loves or a final communion with the spirit of all - so harmful as to be classed a great evil, akin to slavery, and its teaching akin to despotism? Why not simply go on one's way, and leave one's neighbors to believe and worship as they will?

As in this Part I go beyond mere statement of belief and a showing that certain ideas are false, I accept the obligation to justify the right of any person to challenge the beliefs of another. Further, I intend to show this not merely a right, but a duty, when those beliefs include within them an inherent threat, not only to the believer, but to the interests and rights of all.

Were believers in the supernatural to simply believe, and were those who make their living trafficking in myths and magic to go quietly about their trade, others would have little cause to challenge their activities beyond a decent effort to point out erroneous propositions and to minimize the exploitation likely to occasion their propagation. But this is not the case. Churches too often demand belief, and the surrender of money and authority, even from those with no inclination to believe, or who may believe a different way.

They prey also on the desperate, and not only upon those who might judge while at ease and with reason. And while we are regularly urged to see the churches as a comfort to the afflicted, how many have gone to their end in confusion and despair because their prayers have gone unanswered - believing themselves as forsaken by God as the crucified Jesus, or in fear that some unforgiven trespass or secret desire has doomed them to an eternity of torment?

Would it not be more humane to point to the advice of the Lord's Prayer that we seek only acceptance of what is to be than to teach a God who was deaf to the prayers of millions as plagues and blitzkrieg swept across Europe might nonetheless alter the course of nature to extend the life of a single person or interest himself in the payment of a utility bill?

Nor do the churches satisfy themselves attending solely to the concerns of the faithful. They insist upon the indoctrination of children, and the right to frighten and intimidate them into submission with threats of punishment in this world and torture in the hereafter, leaving their victims thoroughly conditioned to accept all manner of baseless propositions, and prone to yield undue authority to those who traffic in mysticism and subvert Reason.

While Mystery, Miracle and Prophecy remain the chief tools of priest-craft, the light of Science has increasingly cleared our vision, and modern claims of supernatural powers are now quickly dismissed by all but the most innocent and naive. So true is this that modern mystics now often attempt disguising their craft by wrapping unreasonable propositions in scientific-sounding language, hiding, as it were, their fanciful notions behind the skirts of Science. But see how quickly they join their more traditional brethren in the attack on Reason when it shows their own doctrines are also without foundation.

Neither do those who claim religious authority demand submission in matters of belief only, for many think themselves entitled to worldly power as well. They appeal to civil government to compel behavior consistent with their own standards from those who do not share them or who do not wish to conform. Whether this is done through a state religion or through other political processes is of little consequence. The effect is the same, and the threat to liberty no less to be feared.

Some will agree this may yet be true, but argue it is in but the extreme cases. Most churches have given up their empires and inquisitions, and no longer seriously threaten the interests of non-believers. These, they argue should be left to themselves. A similar case was made by Burke in his claim that Louis XVI was so gentle and fair a monarch the people of France were unjust to rebel against his rule.

The reply is the same. It was not simply the monarch the French rightly overthrew, it was Hereditary Monarchy, a concept which - like Revealed Religion - includes within its very nature the ever-present threat of despotism. Strip it of its supposed divine authority, deny it a voice in the self-government of the people (and of its power to feed at the public trough), leave all persons free to ignore its proclamations and it matters not if it continues to exist. But if it will not yield this position voluntarily, there is no choice left to freedom-loving people but to see to its removal.

CHAPTER II

THE END OF DEISM

IT IS, I confess, a vanity to imagine some may wonder how my personal views on the subject of Religion might have changed, were I to have knowledge of the events which have taken place in the two centuries since my death. I am emboldened to answer, however, knowing the former Parts of this work are still read, and at present it seems more widely than others of my writings which in their time enjoyed greater acceptance. I proceed in the hope a more current profession of beliefs - and a few words on the process by which they have changed - will satisfy what curiosity may exist, and may be of some use to those following a similar path.

OLD QUESTIONS ANSWERED BY SCIENCE

In his notes on the collection of my writings he published in 1895, Mr. Conway observed some change in my thinking between Part One and Part Two of this work. In the first Part I argued the necessity of belief in a deity based on the then (I believed) unanswerable questions of how else one might explain the existence of Creation itself, but by a Creator, and how else matter might have been put into motion, but by the action of some original Mover. In Part Two I argued additionally the goodness I perceived in human beings, and still perceive, must have originated from the Divine, i.e. without God whence do we gain our moral sense? I have since found the answers to these questions no more mystical - and no less wonderful - than any of my previous observations of the glorious revelations of Nature.

Creation Without a Creator

Two hundred years ago the term Creation was used as a synonym for The Universe, as well as to indicate the presumed process by which it came into being. It was then generally assumed (though it was already understood by some this was not the case) that the Universe as we then perceived it was as it had always been. With no practical theory of origin available to most, and any theory or evidence which might have surfaced brutally suppressed, it was the common wisdom that our intricate, complex and fully developed world had "sprung in completeness" from somewhere and, knowing no other possible explanation, the existence of a Creator must be assumed. As we now know, the underlying assumption has been proved false, and therefore the conclusion is no longer supported.

Among a small number at that time it was already understood the Earth could not possibly have been created whole a mere six thousand years before, as Bishop Uusher had famously calculated. The story of Genesis was not only logically absurd, as I had argued, it was demonstrably false. Beginning with the discoveries of James Hutton, it had been shown the Earth is unimaginably old. Even then it was already understood by some that all forms of life on our planet had evolved from common origins over a gradual process which took millions of years. As these facts are now generally understood, there remains no rational basis upon which to suggest an act of creation as described in Genesis ever occurred. We now know for a fact it did not.

Some who wish to salvage a role for a creator now concede the Earth to be billions of years old, and the Universe billions of years older, but argue that Evolution was simply the process chosen to create life as we know it, i.e. that we were merely mistaken in the past regarding the method, but correct about the Cause. Given what we now know about the process of evolution - relying as it does upon unpredictable events of mutation and sexual interaction, filtered by the resulting advantages in survival and reproduction of those best suited to their current environment - it is absurd to suggest such a process as deliberately chosen to produce what we now perceive to be its end products. Surely if a Creator God wished to make a human or a bear, it would have been within his power to simply do so.

Dependent as it is upon random chance, the actual process of evolution belies any suggestion of deliberate intent. Thus, science has brought us to a place where the delicate, intricate beauty of life on our planet is shown to be infinitely more fragile and complex than we had previously imagined, and at the same time has demonstrated the absence of design (intelligent or otherwise) and left no reason for us to imagine, much less presume, the existence of a Designer.

Matter in Motion

In the eighteenth century I perceived a second proof of the existence of God: matter was *in motion*.[14] At that time what was known of Mechanics had been reduced to a few simple laws, with the implicit understanding that the natural state of matter was a*t rest*. Why then, as could plainly be seen, were the planets and their satellites moving? There was no common theory which might explain why the Earth revolved around the sun, or the moon around the Earth, but that God had made it so.

None would now argue the motion of the planets to be a great mystery. Through Einstein's reflection in his study (and likely also while daydreaming at his job in the Geneva Patent Office) we have come to realize that *motion* is indeed the natural state of matter. From the observations of Hubble, made in his observatory above Pasadena, we have evidence the stars and galaxies are themselves in motion, expanding in all directions away from the central point at which this universe began in a mighty explosion.

Knowing our universe originated in a Big Bang nearly 14 billion years ago has not dissuaded those who seek evidence of a Creator in our emerging knowledge of the cosmos. To the contrary, some find comfort in the notion of such an event, arguing it to be the newly discovered process by which all things were created by God. That this process was revealed by Science, and might well have been discovered much sooner but for the supposedly God-inspired actions of the churches, is routinely overlooked.

Was then the Big Bang merely the physical expression of God saying "Let there be light" or is it possible this event occurred naturally, and may even be one in an ongoing series of such events? While it is impossible to disprove the former proposition, neither can it be supported with evidence or reasoning, nor the latter possibility ruled out. Indeed, as explanations for the existence of the universe continue to be sought in nature, new and increasingly sophisticated theories continue to emerge. Just as the sciences of Geology and Biology, once set free from religious repression, have found for what once were mysteries explanations which point away from a Creator God, so too the sciences of theoretical and astrophysics continue to suggest answers to the origin of the universe which indicate no active role for a divine creator.

A brief aside is warranted here to note that while Science has proved without doubt that life on this planet evolved to its current level of diversity and complexity over many millions of years, and that this process began billions of years after the universe came into existence, nearly half of the American people still appear to believe the world is no more than ten thousand years old. This level of apparent[15] ignorance can be explained only by the privileged position given to religion in American society, which continues to show respect, and even deference, to any idea claimed to be held as a matter of faith, no matter how absurd it may be.

Whence Goodness?

My former editor shares the story of a group of Christian gentlemen debating the extent to which the native people of North America should be treated as human beings, it having been argued they were soulless beasts, more like wild animals than God's European creations who believed themselves invested with immortal souls. This proposition was answered when a native gentleman was brought before the group and asked if he did not feel bad when he did wrong by another, if there was not some inner voice reproving him for having done so. He replied this was, in fact, the case with him, and thereby proved to the satisfaction of the group that he too was endowed by the Creator with an immortal soul.

There was a time when I found this type of reasoning persuasive; when I also believed my conscience to be the voice of God, echoed in the spirit. How, but by an innate moral sense instilled by the Creator could one explain the impulse to do good and avoid evil? Through the work of modern science, we now see that morality, altruism, all of the values we have been taught to believe were God-given, in fact serve important functions in the process of Natural Selection. While these observations do nothing to inform us about the possible existence of God, they do show how these values were developed without the need for any divine intervention, thereby dismantling the last of the pillars which once upheld my own belief in a deity.

Of all the arguments I had heard, and myself made in support of Deism, to the Thomas Paine of 1795, these were the strongest. As I review them in the light of twenty first century knowledge I see them not as arguments at all. Rather, the questions which seemed to me beyond answer two centuries ago have effectively been resolved. This affirms my conviction that unanswered questions do not imply supernatural answers, and my confidence that our remaining questions about the origin of the universe are likely to be resolved in a similar fashion.

Seeing earlier questions answered, my Reason no longer compels me to believe that creation demands a creator or morality a divine source, and rather compels me to acknowledge they do not. While I can imagine no way to disprove the existence of God, as a negative proposition never can be proved, neither can I any longer imagine a proof, or even a compelling argument, for the existence of one. Rather, I now find it impossible to believe that any modern person, were it not for indoctrination during childhood, would ever propose the answer to our remaining questions was likely the existence of an invisible and omnipotent being who created and still controls our universe.

Whatever First Cause I can now imagine, it does not take the form of a being with consciousness and aware of its own existence. Along with that conception, I am forced to surrender remaining belief in any power, knowledge or realm which originates or exists outside of the natural world until such time as I may see evidence - in the true and objective sense – of its existence.

Recognizing, as I now do, no foundation upon which to rest a belief in gods, angels, demons or other spirits, I do not hope for an afterlife, pleasant or otherwise. I know of none other than to be held in the hearts and memory of my countrymen, and in this it appears I have succeeded to a greater degree than most of my former adversaries.

I conclude then it is our Humanity, and not our fear of Divine Judgment, which must drive our moral sense, and our treatment of others. It is this world and no other to which we must direct our attention and our energies.

If, as I have suggested above, Science tells us our moral sense serves a natural purpose, and was likely evolved in the interest of human survival and prosperity, does this sense have somehow less value? To the contrary. Our natural instincts tell us those things which are in our own best interests, and those of our fellow human beings. Further, most of us have little difficulty recognizing which of our instincts are most helpful in a given situation, and when they may need to be contained or redirected for our own or the public good.

For obvious reasons the churches argue against the grounding of morality in Humanity, crediting themselves with the good works carried out and financed by their members. They threaten in anxious desperation that Religion alone is what keeps us from falling into crime and depravity, that without Religion we could not hire enough policemen.

The facts of the case are the opposite. The homicide rate in America, for example, is fifteen times that of Japan, the world's second most atheistic country (after China).[16] In fact, the average homicide rate in the ten most religious countries in the world is nine times that of the ten least religious countries.

Once religiosity is accepted to be without relevance, we are left with only our humanity as the source of our morals, and only our fellow human beings as the proper objects and arbiters of our virtue. Evidence shows that in societies where Humanity is given its proper role Morality flourishes, along with the social policies which most effectively support it. It follows that to do right by ourselves, by humanity as a race, and by our fellow creatures, is the highest moral goal to which we can aspire.

How does a moral system based on Humanity differ from one supposedly based on Divine Inspiration or upon a fear of Divine Judgment? It is, to my mind more principled, more gentle, and more conducive to a way of life compatible with what we understand to be the teachings of Jesus.

If our actions are guided by the good of humanity, we do not need to seek the answers to moral questions in ancient books, or to be commanded by others not to do murder, or to steal the property of another. And unlike those philosophies which claim all other creatures are here for us to exploit, a morality based on Humanity must necessarily recognize our shared interest in the diversity of life and in treating other creatures decently. As Tolstoy has said: "Love, truth, compassion, service, sympathy, tenderness, exist in the hearts of men, and are the essence of religion, but try to encompass these things in an institution and you get a church - and the Church stands for and has always stood for coercion, intolerance, injustice and cruelty. "

THE REALITY OF RELIGIOUS EXPERIENCE

Having reviewed my prior discussion of Missions and Revelations,[17] I note an opportunity to elaborate upon a subject about which much less was then known: that which is called Religious or Spiritual Experience. As I have previously dismissed any duty to accept the claims of revelation made by others, I proceed to review the true origin of the dreams, visions and products of those who believe they have received such revelations, and the benefits derived from what may be called Religious Disciplines.

Despite the commonality of charlatans, it is not to be doubted that some who claim revelatory experiences are sincere, and genuinely believe themselves to have been in direct contact with God, or to otherwise have experienced something supernatural. Clearly profound changes have occurred in the lives of such persons, transforming characters and liberating previously unrecognized qualities. The visions which sometimes occasion these experiences are not to be mistaken for mere psychosis, and are more akin to those sometimes found in epilepsy, or triggered by deliberate efforts to create an altered state of consciousness.

The methods by which this may be achieved have been known for centuries, and vary from one time and culture to another. They cover a wide range, from self-flagellation and fasting to the use of flotation tanks and other forms of sensory deprivation, and the use of drugs such as Peyote, LSD, and Ayahuasca. Similar experiences may result from other types of trauma to the brain, such as are experienced in coma or in what have been called Near Death Experiences.

For those who experience this type of hallucination the perception is usually quite vivid, often taking on an appearance of sharp reality exceeding that found during periods of normal functioning. The after-math frequently includes a transcendent sense of oneness with the world, and a falling away of past ways of viewing reality. A subsequent desire or sense of mission to share the revelation with others often leads to a familiar pattern, inspiring some to follow or emulate visionaries and others to attack and persecute them.

Beneficial results are achieved by many through the practice of spiritual disciplines without entering into a profoundly altered state or experiencing visions. Similarly, some disgorge at length the contents of their subconscious while experiencing nothing more exotic than what seems to them to be a voice in the mind.

Just as we now understand our dreams to be devoid of supernatural content, we can understand that works such as the

Qur'an or *A Course in Miracles* may well seem to their authors to arise from some entirely remote source, but are in fact products of the same subconscious processes. The mystery is to be found not in the fact such things occur, but that they are given supernatural interpretations and turned into the foundation of religions, leading others to spend whole lifetimes searching for the voice of God in sources of purely human origin.

The pleasurable experience of inner peace, oneness with creation - and its imagined Creator - is found by many through disciplines far less shocking to the brain than starving in a cave or taking powerful drugs. Various approaches to prayer, meditation and quiet contemplation have been found effective for this purpose, especially when accompanied by an effort to abandon attempts to regulate one's life or environment through the exercise of conscious will. These, many have noted, are equally effective without regard to a belief that prayers are heard or answered, or whether one meditates upon a flower or the character of the Buddha. A recent variant called Mindfulness Meditation appears to confer similar benefits without a supernatural or religious association of any kind.

As these experiences and disciplines can now be understood, and the knowledge of their true nature grasped by any who wish to attempt them, we can proceed to explore them without succumbing to the delusions of mystics or using them as a foundation upon which to build a structure of supernatural beliefs.

RELIGIOUS FAITH MORE VICE THAN VIRTUE

Given their often demonstrably false claims of supernatural origin, moral superiority and historical accuracy, religious teachings must be seen as more worthy of skepticism than other kinds of thought. This is addition-ally true because most religious ideas have been so constructed and transmitted as to rely upon the demand of submission to authority and upon misleading interpretations of reality to overcome the natural protests of reason.

Though a healthy skepticism is essential to social and economic success in a free society, churches teach against this to serve their own ends, offering instead a variety of psychological palliatives and in-group supports, typically paired with the teaching of fear and hostility towards those regarded as infidels. Thus, religion has long served to enfeeble the intellect of believers and as a justification for all manner of evils directed toward those who differ in their beliefs, gender, skin color, or sexuality from those of the dominant group.

Is it to be argued then that religious belief and observance, or the practice of spiritual disciplines should be restrained? Should we be bar-red from prayer in times of trial, or of the company of others in the search for truth and meaning? Decidedly not.

As we have seen, prayer, meditation and quiet contemplation, however practiced, hold genuine benefits for the practitioner. The teaching of these practices, devoid of mystical attachments, should be part of every modern program of health education, along with current information on exercise and nutrition. If all so instructed were also educated to the predictable pitfalls of seeking objective truths on the path of inner experience, and in the use of reason to avoid them, it seems they would be better equipped to cope with normal human experience.

Were this accompanied by education in the principles of all philosophies, including atheism and humanism along with the traditional religions,[18] and especially with instruction in the absolute right of all persons to be free from coercion in matters of belief, it could be said a person's religious education was complete. Contrast this with the common approach to religious *indoctrination* practiced by the churches.

In return for the offer of comfort in times of trouble, and supportive fellowship throughout life, the churches demand a high price. First, one is told to abandon skepticism, and to refrain from the use of reason, substituting instead a blind faith in the authority of others and their questionable interpretations of nature and of history. No other interpretations are to be considered or believed, and punishment may be expected by those bold enough to do so. Next, one must submit one's self and one's children to extended indoctrination in ideas which defy logic, and which for the most part serve no useful purpose, as example or otherwise. Lastly, one must contribute from even meager resources to the support of a class of showmen – for they are almost always men - who are trained primarily in the telling of stories, and skilled principally in the arts of deceiving the mind. Failure to submit will bring immediate social and economic costs within the community, and likely also the threat of eternal torture in the imagined afterlife. Can there be any doubt of the unwholesome effects of such a process?

The age is upon us when we can understand what is useful and harmful in the teaching of religious ideas. It has, for example, been shown the act of prayer is beneficial for the one who prays, while having no effect whatever on the course of nature. Let us take this example as a lesson on how we can preserve what has been learned from the practices of the faithful to benefit humanity while freeing ourselves and our fellow citizens from the burdens of supernatural mysticism.

As for the priests, missionaries and gurus: let those who know a useful discipline or technique for bringing peace and insight to others teach it, and let them be paid their worth. Let those who have ideas on how others should live their lives speak freely, publish as they will, and receive whatever return society gives them. Let them also pay their taxes - as must their benefactors - on their own incomes and places of business. But let no person claim authority over the mind or body of another and justify this with the supposed demand or sanction of some mythical Higher Power. All such claims are false, and deserve the hostility and rejection of all.

CHAPTER III

THE SCRIPTURES REVISITED

IN THE years since my death, progress has been made by historians leading to a greater understanding of Jesus and his times, and of the events related to the organization of the Christian church by the Roman Emperor Constantine. I begin this Chapter with a brief summary of what is now known, and how it reflects upon the prior Parts of this work.

Inspired by the belief that under the sign of Christ he would be more successful in bringing death to his enemies, Constantine converted to Christianity and soon set about bringing Roman organization to the widely scattered and diverse factions which then remained of the movement started by Jesus. Jerusalem, the original center of Jesus' sect, had long since been destroyed by Roman forces, along with what was left of the core leadership. Most of what had survived were small communities established by Jesus' disciples, and those which had been converted to the unique brand of Christianity preached by Paul, the self-appointed apostle to the Gentiles.

Though Paul had never met Jesus, he nonetheless thought of himself as similar to those who had been with him throughout his ministry. Paul's teachings were rejected by Jesus' successor - his brother James - and by the other leaders of the Church at Jerusalem. So much so they sent their own missionaries to congregations started by Paul to correct his doctrines.

Most importantly, Paul taught that Jesus was God, and that belief in this alone was required for salvation. This teaching

was denied by the Jerusalem authorities, who remained practicing Jews until their deaths. They taught that action according to the instruction and example of Jesus was required in
addition to belief; as James said, that faith without works is
dead.

Paul's ideas were nonetheless accepted by many, but by no
means all Christians left after the destruction of Jerusalem.
There were groups who believed then, as now, that Jesus was
not God, and had simply died. Some evidently believed he had
escaped crucifixion altogether. Others believed the story of his
death and resurrection, and with varying doctrines and
expectations awaited Jesus' return. Those who believed in his
divinity debated if he had always been God, or was literally a
son of God, in the manner of those said to be the product of
Greek and Roman gods mating with human women.

Following the council of bishops that Constantine himself
called and chaired at Nicaea in 325 CE, the Pauline version of
Christianity became the authorized doctrine of the Roman
church, and all other sects were (sometimes brutally) suppressed, their scriptures destroyed. Paul's somewhat anti-
Semitic and Roman-friendly brand of Christianity found a
receptive audience in the Empire, and even if his writings
were not originally more numerous, they constitute most of
what survived the purges which followed Constantine's demand for organization of the faith.

For centuries following, the Roman church, like the cult of
Jerusalem temple priests before it, maintained an alliance with
civil government in their mutual efforts to suppress all who
challenged the authority of Church or State. The irony that it
was precisely this type of institutional partnership which
brought Jesus into fatal conflict with the then-existing estab-
lishment in Palestine seems to have been lost on Christians
since the founding of the Church of Rome.

Despite the unearthing of new documents and the birth of a
new science of Archeology, no findings of researchers made
since their publication have refuted any of the arguments
presented in the earlier Parts of this work. While the discoveries of the Rosetta Stone and the Nag Hamaddi library serve to

undermine some of the claims of Joseph Smith and the Pauline Christians, no evidence of any kind has surfaced in the last two hundred years to imply the slightest support for the fantastic fables I have previously debunked. Most obviously, Jesus has failed to meet the many predicted dates for his return to Earth, which began with the clear statements in the gospels that this miraculous event would occur during the lives of those then present. No evidence of a great flood has been found, and it can now be shown the population of the earth numbered in the millions - and has done so continuously - since long before the time of Creation calculated by Bishop Uusher.

I wish to note here a recent commentary[19] suggesting that in preparing Part One of this work I may have characterized incorrectly the role of Satan in the story of Genesis. There is indeed no indication the serpent of that fable was one and the same with the most reviled of the angels, and neither the name of Satan nor the one mistakenly given to him in the King James version (Lucifer)[20] appears in Genesis.

To whatever or whomever the serpent of Genesis was, while still able to speak and not yet crawling on the ground, the Old Testament gives us no clue. It is not until we reach Jude and Revelations (where most of the current Christian mythology regarding Satan and his exploits appears to have begun) that we find the serpent of Genesis identified with Satan. It is this conflation by Christian mythologists to which I have directed earlier commentary on this subject, and not to the actual words of Genesis.

This discussion has attracted my attention to a subject upon which I made only passing comment in the earlier Parts, but which now seems to me more important in light of recent reports suggesting the surprising resiliency of myths about angels and demons.[21]

Angels and Demons

I noted in Part Two, the use of the word Satan as a proper name appears only once with certainty in the Old Testament, in the Book of Job. In this remarkable story, Satan appears at a gathering of "the sons of God" (which term goes without explaination). Subjected to boasting by the deity regarding the extraordinary piety of Job, whom He considers the most virtuous of men, Satan replies with taunts, successfully needling God to agree this most excellent man should be subjected to torture and ruin to prove the accuracy of God's assessment of his virtue. In this story, Satan appears more an agent or familiar of God sent to test the fidelity of his human creation, than as some sort of fallen angel and enemy of the deity.

As I also noted in Part Two, the personification of The Adversary likely originates outside of Hebrew tradition, as does the myth of Satan's prideful refusal to bow to Man as the cause of his supposed downfall, which is the accepted story in Islam. I have also discussed before[22] Satan's reported appearance to Jesus after he fasted in the desert, and the events which supposedly took place between them. As they were said to be the only ones present, and as we are assured the Evangelists did not use Satan as their source, we must assume the story was first told by Jesus or that it was fabricated by others.

I remain reluctant to believe Jesus would tell such a story. If he did indeed report an experience of this kind, it would certainly be compatible with what are now known to be the effects of sensory deprivation, and the sort of biochemical derangement one might expect while fasting alone for weeks in the deserts of Palestine.

There are, of course, numerous references in the Bible to demonic possessions and exorcisms, involving persons who appear to the modern eye to be suffering from some form of psychosis or epilepsy. While belief in such possessions persists in some cultures, like miracles and all other supernatural events they fail to appear where science and skepticism are enough present to reveal natural causes and trickery.

Unlike Satan and his minions, about whom we do not hear again until we reach the end of the New Testament, godly messengers appear throughout the scriptures of all Abrahamic religions. They are endowed with various characteristics and powers, depending upon their assignment. Such messengers, for example, appear at Lot's door, after Abraham had succeeded – to no useful purpose - in negotiating with God a 90% reduction in the number of righteous souls it would take to save Sodom and Gomorrah from destruction.

When the Sodomites come looking to sodomize Lot's visitors – who later show themselves powerful enough to blind the aggressors and destroy their cities – these angels stay behind the door while Lot pleads for their safety, inviting the crowd to instead rape his two virgin daughters – the same daughters who will later bear Lot's other children. In this way we are given an early introduction to Old Testament morality of both men and angels.

In most subsequent appearances these messengers deliver their announcements and move on. Some make their appearance only in dreams, such as the one who informed Joseph that Mary had conceived her pregnancy by supernatural means, and not by a Roman soldier called Panthera as later Jewish writings suggest.

This is all the Bible has to tell us of these creatures until we arrive on the island of Patmos where John[23] had his Revelations while "in the spirit." The elaborately detailed rankings and powers of the angels, as imagined by Christian mystics and "angelologists" find no real basis in scripture.

In consulting the work of the learned Dr. Billy Graham on this subject,[24] a book which has reportedly sold millions of copies in America alone, he is found as ignorant of his Bible as he is confident in the reality of these imagined creatures. His work may be recommended, however, as an example of the amount of detail Christian mythologists can wring from a few phrases in the Old Testament and the hallucinations of a man living alone on a Greek island.

Here I end my discussion of the great book of fables, and introduce two other critiques - one subtle and the other somewhat less so – which may be of interest to the reader.

Mr. Jefferson's Bible

I begin with a word about the religious beliefs of Thomas Jefferson. I had the honor of knowing Jefferson well, and of working with him on several important projects. While my own role in the drafting of our Declaration of Independence has been exaggerated in some quarters, it cannot be doubted Mr. Jefferson collaborated with many others, myself included, in exploring the philosophies which are the foundation of our claim of independence from England and for the constitution of our government.

Jefferson was for a time our Minister to France, during which period we continued our friendship, and on my return to America I was his guest for some months. During his Presidency I had the opportunity to advise him on certain matters pertaining to relations with France. It is widely and accurately reported that my advice in these matters in part led to the (Louisiana) purchase of a vast area of land from Napoleon's government, opening the door to the continent-wide republic we had envisioned since Revolutionary times. I mention these things not to celebrate my own role in historic events, but simply to show my familiarity with Jefferson and his philosophy was broad-based and first-hand.

As with all great men, advocates of one position or another have from the beginning claimed that Jefferson held to the same beliefs they wished to impress upon others, either positively or negatively. Most such efforts are in vain. Jefferson was, by his own accurate description, a sect of one who questioned everything, including the existence of God.[25]

While it is true Jefferson was a man of strong principles and beliefs, it is also fair to say he sometimes failed to demonstrate these through his actions. With respect to expressing his religion, he was not only inconsistent in this way, he was reticent to the point of near-opacity. Always under attack by religious conservatives, Jefferson had a practical need to be cautious in his public statements just as politicians in the present time must still appear pious. The Constitution's prohibition of any religious test for public office was as much ignored by the public then as it is now.

The fact Jefferson belonged to no Christian church nearly cost him his turn at the Presidency. During the campaign of 1800 he was pilloried by his enemies for his lack of religious beliefs, (most accurately) labeled a Deist and often (inaccurately) called an Atheist. After an electoral tie with Aaron Burr, it was the House of Representatives that gave the Presidency to Jefferson. During his time in office, and even thereafter, he kept his true religious beliefs secret from all but a few trusted intimates, and did his best to maintain the appearance of a pious believer. The complexity of Jefferson's behavior with regard to religion is illustrated by a familiar tale:

I have seen repeated by several authors a story about Jefferson and his religious beliefs. In some cases the story is attributed to Ethan Allen. In other versions Jefferson speaks to an unnamed friend, a stranger, or a journalist. In each version the President is on his way to Sunday morning services, and carries under his arm a book bound in red leather, reported as either a Bible or a large prayer book. His opposite in the encounter chides him in reference to the book, saying "You don't believe a word of it." In some versions Jefferson responds that no nation has ever held together without religion, and as chief magistrate it was his duty to maintain one.

Of course, Jefferson actually believed it was his duty to maintain a Wall of Separation between Church and State (it was he who coined the phrase) though he recognized the necessity of keeping peace with religious believers and of thwarting antagonists who would use religion as a political weapon against him. The more important aspect of the story, however, is the red book seen under Jefferson's arm. There most definitely was such a book and it did, in fact, reflect Jefferson's deeply held religious beliefs!

The existence of Jefferson's *The Philosophy of Jesus* was known to few during his lifetime. The volume was bound in red leather with gold trim and title inscription and was purchased by Jefferson with blank pages. In the course of a few evenings, while serving as President of the United States, Jefferson fashioned the content of his book by cutting passages from copies of bibles printed in English and Greek, and pasting them side by side in its pages. He included only passages which directly reflected the teachings of Jesus as reported by the New Testament evangelists, blending the four gospels in chronological order, and excluding any passage referring to the supernatural. There is no reference to virgin birth, resurrection, or any of the miracles said to be performed by Jesus.

This thoroughly scrambled and redacted version of the gospels he found to contain the most sublime philosophy ever given to man. It allowed him to truthfully claim to be a Christian in what he called the only way that mattered: he believed in, if he did not always follow, the teachings of Jesus.

It is not my intent to criticize Mr. Jefferson for the evident hypocrisy in his efforts to hide his religious beliefs or for the much more grievous facts surrounding his enslavement of other human beings. Like many great men, he championed the ideals to which he aspired, for himself and for humanity. Nor do I mean to judge him harshly for his practicality in seeking to avoid the bludgeon of religion ever wielded by his enemies, for it appears Jefferson's place in history has been preserved by his success in evading their blows. What was wrong then, as it is now, is that religion played any role whatever in the fortunes or career of an American political leader and public servant.

The Bible and Human Rights

I have previously noted the consistency with which religion has been used by tyrants as a weapon against progress, and by churches as a tool with which to manipulate and exploit the common people. Always happy to make a comfortable home for themselves in the shadow of kings and princes, practitioners of the priestly trade have ever been adept at finding in the Bible passages to justify the most heinous of crimes.

For centuries those who would challenge royal authority were promised not only certain death in this world, but divine punishment in the next. In return for their collaboration, religious states have rewarded the churches with suppression of free thought and free speech, keeping the people in ignorance and maintaining the monopoly of the church over the concessions attending birth, marriage, death, and the search for inner peace.

From the time of Constantine until the American Revolution, religious heresy was equated in every way with sedition, and Bible teachings used to justify the lash, the noose and the stake. Since those times the cause of Human Rights has expanded and progressed in many ways, however slowly and unevenly. The past two centuries have seen great movements at social reform, most importantly in America the movements for equality by African Americans and women, and more recently the movement for freedom in sexual expression. At each new turn, religious authorities have been there to sanction the predations of the tyrants, and to promise pie in the sky for those who bear their oppression in graceful silence.

As I have shown the ancient scriptures to be lacking in credibility or moral authority, I am inclined to dismiss without comment the protestations of those who would say the holy books authorize the enslavement of human beings, the subjugation of women, or the denial of rights on account of which myths people believe or the gender of their lovers. I see no purpose in arguing specific applications of false doctrines. If one's conscience does not say it is wrong to enslave, no argument from Thomas Paine will make the case. And, as Gerrit Smith once said: "What too, if, as is held by many, Paul does teach that woman as compared with man is an inferior order of being? - who that receives such insane teaching is fit to have a wife or a daughter?"[26]

While I personally feel no impulse to challenge the duplicity of the religious friends of oppression, I would call the reader's attention to one particularly masterful exercise of this type:

Mrs. Stanton's Bible

Some may recall the World Anti-Slavery Convention held in London in 1840. There, William Lloyd Garrison, who was the acknowledged leader of the movement in America, refused to speak or take his honored place on the floor of the Convention while the women delegates in attendance were confined to a balcony and forbidden to speak (and this nearly 50 years after Mary Wollstonecraft had published her *Vindication of the Rights of Women*!).

More important to the cause of Human Rights than the actions of Garrison or any of the proceedings at that convention was the fateful meeting there of Elizabeth Cady Stanton and her future collaborator, Lucretia Mott. For it was there the seeds were sown for the meeting held eight years later at Seneca Falls to address the Rights of Woman in America. Here we mark the beginning of the great nineteenth century American movement to liberate women from oppressive laws, and to the attainment of their full equal rights, a movement which like our American Revolution has greatly advanced the cause of freedom for women and men around the world.

Like the then-ongoing effort to abolish Slavery in America, the movement for Woman's Rights was vigorously opposed by conservative forces, aided by oppressive laws and a clergy quick to cite biblical authority for the permanent subjugation of all women. While that movement had true friends among the male population, few of our gender made the cause of women their highest priority. There were, of course, exceptions such as Parker Pillsbury and African American leaders such as Charles Redmond and the great Frederick Douglass, who saw an interest in the freedom and equality of all to be the equal moral obligation of every American. For the most part, however, the women were left to fight for the cause unaided.

After a long and bloody civil war, the question of Slavery was forever settled in America, and the slow march toward equal rights for African-Americans began. As more widespread attention then focused on the freedom of women, they achieved victories against the most egregious denials of their rights in property, their children and in their own persons. A crucial battle could be seen in the then not distant future for the right to vote. Susan B. Anthony, having set that goal as her main point of navigation, made her alliance with conservative forces which sought votes for women in hopes of establishing America as an officially Christian nation.

Stanton, by contrast, wanted none of this, and saw increasingly the institutional opposition of the churches as the primary obstacle to full freedom for women. As the end of her career approached, Stanton made use of the skills she had developed with Mott, to launch a new project in which the supposed support of the Bible for the subjugation of woman was blasted. She called her project *The Woman's Bible*.

Addressing herself to her sisters, it served her purpose not to reject the Bible outright. Instead Mrs. Stanton, working with a committee of advisers and her scholarly collaborator Matilda Joslyn Gage, proceeded to show which women in the Bible stories provided examples worthy of emulation, and how many acquitted themselves favorably (and usually in a morally superior way)to their male counterparts. And so she makes her case, leaving her readers to judge if the stories are true, but relieving them nonetheless of any authority to support the denial of woman's equal rights.

As in my own case, it may have been wise for Mrs. Stanton to have waited until the end of her political career to address directly the role of the churches in restraining human progress. It appears that she developed her full appreciation of that role through the long progress of her career, noting in each battle the constant presence of at least one constant enemy on the field. Be that as it may, no sooner had she announced her project than she was attacked as infidel, and either in sympathy with that sentiment or in fear of its consequences, many of her remaining former allies withdrew from her. She ended her career always pressing for a broader social and philosophical program, while the movement she helped to catalyze, increasingly focused on Suffrage, left her behind.

The Final Testament

Over the past century, events in the Middle East and their global consequences have increased the importance that every American under-stand the religion of Islam in at least a fundamental way. I undertake a brief statement toward this end, as I have noted that among Americans I encounter, most lack even the most basic awareness of the teachings of Muhammad, and their relation to those of other religions. I offer the following as but the briefest of summaries, and urge the reader to explore further as may be indicated.

The third of the so-called Great or Abrahamic Religions, the birth of Islam follows that of Christianity by hundreds of years. The revelations then claimed by Muhammad – first brought to him in visions by the Angel Gabriel while meditating in his favorite cave – consequently reflect what had gone before. They embraces many of the older traditions, accepting the Jewish creation myth, belief in angels, and recognizing the Jewish prophets (including Jesus and his virgin birth). It denies others, for example the notion of the Trinity, and calls into question if Jesus was actually crucified at all, or if another died in his place. In Islam, Muhammad is seen as the Final Prophet, and the Qur'an as the Final Testament.

The Qur'an is a collection of Muhammad's teachings, sometimes committed to memory by his followers and some-times inscribed on whatever was available while he was delivering his revelations. It was collected into a book within a few decades of his death by those who had served as his scribes and closest disciples. The book itself is therefore, in this regard, somewhat more likely an accurate record of Muhammad's sayings than is the New Testament with respect to Jesus.

Like other prophets Muhammad did not initially receive a warm reception where he was already known, and so he moved to another city where the claims of an illiterate merchant to be a messenger from Allah found greater acceptance. Like other prophets to follow, Muhammad taught Islam was the restoration of the true religion of Abraham, correcting the errors of Jewish and Christian biblical scribes. Unlike most prophets, he ultimately succeeded in raising an army and returned to conquer his homeland, ultimately unify-ing the Arabian peninsula under the banner of Islam.

Muslims are taught to pray multiple times per day and to submit entirely to the will of Allah (which they consider the personal name of God in Arabic, as Yahweh is in Hebrew, according to the Jews). As in other religions, the disciplines of willful surrender and frequent prayer create a strong positive effect, reinforcing the conviction of the devout they are on the right path, and therefore their acceptance of their prophet's teachings.

Like most Christians, Muslims are taught to believe there will be a final Judgment Day in which all will be dispatched to either Paradise or Hell Fire. In rejecting the Trinity and the divinity of Jesus, Muslims share common ground with Unitarians. In their obligation to perform good works in addition to having faith, they hew more closely to the teachings of the early Jewish Christians than do many contemporary followers of the Pauline variety.

Having inherited virtually all the faults of the Bible, the Qur'an has left Islam in much the same position as Christianity and Judaism: having some worthwhile ideas, but founded on a platform of ancient superstition which can no longer be taken seriously, and consequently devoid of authority in any matter involving contemporary human affairs. In their explicit hostility toward Jews, the teachings of Muhammad established a lasting platform for conflict which is unlikely to be resolved until both sides recognize their differences are fabricated from the imaginations of men long dead.

While Muslims may regard Mohammad as the Final Prophet, in both Eastern and Western cultures the prophets and their testaments have kept coming. Since the founding of Islam around 600 CE, Christianity, Judaism and Islam itself have fragmented into various sects, reflecting philosophical divisions and struggles over leadership, recalling the state of affairs following the death of Jesus, and foreshadowing events following the outbreak of new religions in America in the first half of the nineteenth century.

CHAPTER FOUR

THE NEW RELIGIONS

MILLERISM, MORMONISM AND THE PERSISTENCE OF BELIEF

IN THE years following the Revolution, America began its westward expansion into frontier areas previously populated by few white people. In the economically depressed period following the War of 1812, increasingly factional religious movements spread throughout my adopted home state, reaching as far as Rochester and Buffalo. There followed a period of religious revival in which the region was criss-crossed by traveling preachers, each spreading his or her own revelation and path to salvation. While Catholics and Unitarians remained despised minorities, the people of Western New York (then meaning west of the Catskills) were receptive to all manner of Protestant denominations and itinerant evangelists.

So often had the fires of religious revival swept over the area, it came to be called the Burned Over District. In this region there developed numerous religious sects, and later, along what is now Interstate 90 between Buffalo and Boston, the centers of the 19th century movements to abolish slavery and advance the rights of women.

It was during these times that two religious sects were founded which hold particular interest. The first was initiated by Joseph Smith, a young Vermonter who started claiming religious experiences and mystical powers at the age of fourteen, after his family was driven by hard times to relocate to the area between Rochester and Syracuse. The other, also a millennialist faction, attracted supporters from New England to Ohio to William Miller's proclamation the return of Jesus was imminent. The stories of these two groups illustrate important facts about how religious beliefs persist, and continues to spread, despite irrefutable proof they are wholly and completely false.

Much like Bishop Uusher before him, Miller thought he had discovered previously unknown facts through careful study and calculations based on revelations he found in the Bible. After a year and a half of uncertainty, he ultimately specified the date in October 1844 on which Christ would return, and judgment be pronounced.

Believers in Miller's teachings obtained the largest revival tent until then ever seen, and traveled the region holding massive rallies to warn disbelievers and to prepare the faithful. This went on from spring of 1843 until the Fall of 1844, when the appointed day finally arrived. That day came to be known among believers and critics alike as the Great Disappointment.

Unlike Bishop Uusher, Miller lived to see his theory disproved, and the devastating impact on many of his followers. Forced to explain Jesus' failure to appear as expected, Miller concluded the second coming had in fact occurred unnoticed and that Judgment Day was past. This had unforeseen results, as some of the faithful - convinced they were now immortal and past further judgment - proceeded to comport themselves in embarrassing ways.

While some remnants of Millerism survive in the sect known as the Seventh Day Adventists, most factions disappeared, their adherents moving on to other prophets and the growing Universalist movement. The few Adventists who remained following the Great Disappointment are now greatly outnumbered by the Mormons, whose presence in America appears[27] approximately equal to that of the Jews.

Academic researchers continue to study the Book of Mormon, and to speculate about the process by which it may have been compiled.[28] Sole authorship is commonly attributed to Joseph Smith, the self-described prophet whose reported obsession with Bible study may account for the almost comically King James-ish language which pervades the work.

Other theories suggest the direct involvement of the Baptist preacher Sidney Rigdon, along with a few of Smith's close associates, likely with apparent inspiration from others' prior works in addition to the Bible. One of these, like the Book of Mormon, incorporated elements of local myths attributed to the people indigenous to the area where Smith lived.

The Book of Mormon is based on a story which could not at the time of its publication be verified, but whose authenticity can now be dismissed in at least four ways: there is no credible evidence the claimed ancient source document ever existed; the method by which Smith claims to have translated the story from a book of ancient hieroglyphs has nonetheless been proved invalid; the civilization described in the book never existed, nor did the means by which it supposedly found itself in North America;[29] and finally it can be shown beyond doubt that persons identified as the living descendants of those told of in the book in fact are not. As the book can thus be shown a fraud, it matters little to our discussion from what other works of fiction, or by whom, it may have been plagiarized.

The Golden Book

According to Smith, he received the Book of Mormon in the form of golden plates inscribed with hieroglyphs and connected with metal rings. These plates were shown to him by a "resurrected person" by the name of Moroni who had become an angel and who, according to Smith, wrote some of the book's contents while still a living man. This angel, he says, visited Smith three times in the same night during which he related each time the identical story of his lost civilization and its history inscribed in a book of golden plates, returning to heaven in a beam of light between visits.

After being kept awake the whole night, Smith was unable to work and collapsed in a field the next day, where he was once again visited by Moroni, who repeated the story again, but this time authorized Smith to tell it to his father, who was present at the time. Joseph's father, we are told, immediately believed, though he apparently saw no angel.

According to Smith he was shortly allowed to see the plates where they were buried in a nearby hill, but was required to wait four years before taking them home to be translated, using devices found with them which made him into a "seer" - a notion entirely consistent with his previous claims.

While Smith's stories of visions and supernatural sight had previously gotten him into trouble,[30] similar claims were common in his circle. His principal assistant in its supposed translation - Oliver Cowdery - also claimed he had visions of the Golden Book, both before and after its discovery. Another of Smith's associates, Hiram Page, similarly claimed to receive revelations from God through use of a magic stone until Smith ordered he desist, after which Page's stone was ground to dust and the records of his revelations burned. Others of Smith's associates claimed similar powers and revelations both before and after the end of his life.

The Golden Book, arguably the most important artifact in Western history, were it to exist, is nowhere to be found. According to Smith, after he translated the book through a process which did not even require him to be in the same room, it was returned to the Angel Moroni and once again hidden. Ruled as it is by a group of businessmen,[31] it is not surprising the Church of Jesus Christ of Latter Day Saints expends no resources in searching for it.

The claimed existence of the Golden Book and the story it tells are so obviously implausible, the Book of Mormon actually begins with an acknowledgment of its incredibility, and immediately asks the reader to suspend the use of reason and instead to "ponder it in their hearts" and to ask God - in faith - if it is true.

To bolster his claim, Smith provides attestations to the existence of the Golden Book by a small number of people - about the same number as attested to Jesus' resurrection - mostly related to one another and to Smith. We find on the list three Smiths including Joseph's father and brothers, four Whitmers and Hiram Page, the aforementioned seer (who was also married to a Whitmer). Three others attest to the existence of the book on the basis of having seen it in visions, including

Oliver Cowdery (the same who also claimed he saw it in a vision before Smith dug it up) and who transcribed Smith's "reading" of the plates but was not allowed to see them in the common meaning of the word, and Martin Harris, who financed the initial publication of the book. Were one inclined to initially accept the possibility of the Golden Book's existence, seeing the methods used to convince the reader of its authenticity should alone extinguish the thought.

As there is much to suggest benign intent on Smith's part, at least in the early chapters of his story, it is reasonable to suspect the Book of Mormon a pious fraud[32] by Smith and others to lend unique qualities of mystery and miracle to Smith's claims of prophecy. Should there remain any doubts regarding the actual existence of the Golden Book, these are blasted as we move on to Smith's reported process of translation.

Translation

According to the Book of Mormon, the original writing was in "Reformed Egyptian" a language known only among its authors' race, of which Moroni was the last survivor. In consequence, only a supernatural process would have allowed Smith to translate its text. Thus, according to the tale, one was provided in the form of a contraption incorporating two magic stones found along with the Golden Book.

As the supposed original is nowhere to be found, we are unable to verify the characters in it represent an otherwise unknown language or the accuracy of Smith's mystical translation. Fate, however, has provided a near perfect substitute.

Sometime after publishing the Book of Mormon, Smith published another work titled *The Book of Abraham*,[33] translated, he said, from ancient papyri he purchased in 1835 from a dealer in curiosities and using, according to those present, the same method with which he had previously translated the Book of Mormon. After Smith's death some of these papyri came into the possession of the Metropolitan Museum in New York, where years later they were determined to be common Egyptian funerary scrolls dated from the first century

CE. Despite all manner of explanations by the Church, the evident truth is that Smith ultimately did know what Egyptian writing looked like, and most definitely did not know how to translate it.

That his *Book of Abraham* is in no way related to the source documents from which it supposedly came stands as proof Smith's process of translation was invalid. Consequently, were any Golden Book to have existed, we can reasonably expect Smith's "translation" to be likewise spurious.[34]

The Missing Civilization

The Book of Mormon tells the tale of an ancient civilization created in the Western Hemisphere by people who sailed here from Jerusalem in the year 600 BCE, replacing a still earlier group which supposedly came to America in the mythical diaspora described in the story of the Tower of Babel. After a great war, the later civilization was destroyed and all that were left were the Lamanites, said to be ancestors of the current indigenous people of this hemisphere.

While some Mormon believers have reportedly spent a lifetime searching for the remains of Moroni's Nephite culture, no such remains exist. A vast and sophisticated civilization of well-armed warriors which existed throughout the Western Hemisphere a few thousand years before, one which engraved books on metal plates, is gone without a single trace. Yet throughout North and South America we have the remains of other humans - and their cultural artifacts - going back at least ten thousand years.

As with the missing Golden Book, it appears the Mormon Church funds no archaeological expeditions in search of the lost civilization. It does however still perpetuate the myth through programming on its privately owned cable network, in which ancient ruins of actual early American cultures are misidentified as belonging to the lost civilization. Independent entrepreneurs also make a business of guiding gullible Mormons on tours of such sites.

That no trace of a pre-Christian Semite culture can be found in the Americas is not surprising, considering the hemisphere would not be reached by Vikings for another sixteen hundred years, and by other Europeans for an additional five hundred, after these people supposedly arrived on ships from Jerusalem. Even if Thor Heyerdahl had been correct about the possibility of Egyptian ocean travel on boats made of reeds, there was no approach to shipbuilding known in 600 BCE (much less hundreds of years before) which could have accomplished the migrations reported in the book published by Smith.

Though the point may be obvious, I shall note here that if there was no Nephite civilization it follows then there were no authors for the Golden Book, nor resurrected beings become angels available to deliver it.

The Lamanites

According to Mormon doctrine, all Native Americans are descended from the surviving Lamanites, their dark skin a sign of their degraded condition in the eyes of God. While the church officially abandoned its demonization of Africans in 1978, in the 21st century it is still not uncommon for tradition-al Mormon believers to refer to the native people of this country as Lamanites, presumably still believing, as Joseph Smith taught, that if they embrace Mormon teachings they will someday turn white.

Far more damning than the absence of physical or logical support for the missing civilization has been the emergence of positive genetic evidence of the origin of all indigenous people of the Western Hemisphere. It has been shown that all are descended from people who migrated over land from Siberia, and reached North America at least ten thousand years ago. Simply, there is physical proof the story of a migration from Jerusalem cannot be true.

The history of the church founded by Joseph Smith is a sad and sordid one, the details of which are available to any who wish to learn them. However, no further study is needed to show, as I have above, that it is founded upon a fraud.

Were it not for the obviously fabulous tale of the Golden Book, and were it to be believed Smith was indeed the author, it would be fair to allow he was perhaps unaware of the true origin of his revelations, and that he might simply have been unable to recognize their source as being within himself. In light of what is shown however, this seems too great a charity to expect of any thoughtful person.

The Persistence of Belief

How then are we to understand a church built upon such a foundation, proclaimed (like so many others) to be formed in the last days before the return of Christ, to still be with us after nearly 200 years, propagated around the world, powerful in public affairs and the owner of a vast business empire which includes television stations, newspapers and shopping malls? How is one to explain the continued adherence of modern, educated men and women to religious teachings which are plainly, manifestly untrue?

In the first instance it is evident Joseph Smith set out with the intent to found a religion, that he drew upon the teachings and traditions that he knew, and incorporated into his work much that was familiar, accepted and idealistic in the religious thoughts of the time. He preached a gospel of importance to Americans (which supported their prejudices toward the native people around them) and incorporated all the aspects of the supernatural which suited his visionary character. He also emphasized the nearness of the end of days, which was a popular belief at that time, and lent urgency to those seeking a right path to avoid being left behind. Like other prophets before and since, he claimed he was re-establishing at God's command the original religion of Abraham, including the Aaronic Priesthood. These things aided Smith in the gaining of converts, though similar to the experience of Jesus and others, the prophet initially found a warmer reception as he moved away from where he was already well known.

Secondly, the strangeness of Mormon doctrines, rituals[35] and sexual practices, their separateness, and the success they demonstrated in pursuing an orderly, pious and industrious program all no doubt conspired with the skepticism and jealousy of others, and with the obvious flaws in Smith's personal character, to provoke hostility and then violence wherever they settled. Already inclined to exclusivity, and to see themselves as the moral superiors of their neighbors, the reactions they met created martyrs and further strengthened their resolve to survive and prevail.

Thirdly, after the mobbing and murder of Joseph Smith and his brother Hyrum, the removal to the remote Utah territory under the leadership of the autocratic Brigham Young created an environment in which the church could develop without interference, and using the full powers of the Territorial Government. Free from attack by better armed neighbors, utterly dependent upon one another, and subject to the religious and governmental authority of their new prophet, Mormons' great accomplishments and great embarrassments were free to propagate for years under an absolute theocracy.

I lastly refer the reader to the point made in Chapter One of this Part regarding the methods by which churches prevent free thought, and their effects on the minds and character of those exposed to these methods. There is no greater example of this in American history than that of the Mormons in the Utah Territory and its remaining presence there, and around the world.

Any reasonable person can imagine how a band of migrants kept under strict - sometimes violent - authoritarian control in a remote desert, with virtually no access to outside information, constantly reminded they are despised by others and believing themselves in constant danger, would turn inward. In such an environment the Jews of the Old Testament believed themselves the chosen of God as they supposedly wandered the Middle East committing unspeakable atrocities, and similarly did the Mormons in the remote environment of the Utah Territory. Under such conditions one can understand how many failed to see or escape the tragic contradictions in the leadership of Brigham Young, even when made by them into murderers, thieves and kidnappers, as they were at Circleville and the Mountain Meadow.

After the church leaders were stripped of civil authority, and its members compelled to abandon their signature polygamy or face forfeiture of the church's resources, Mormons retained many of their earlier practices. Their well developed techniques for indoctrinating members and keeping apostates away from the faithful find few parallels elsewhere in American religion, and none so close as those used by the Church of Scientology.[36] This is especially true among fundamentalists who continue to follow the Patriarchs in their treatment of wives and daughters, some of whom can still be found locked away until given - often while still children - in arranged marriages to men two and three times their age. The more extreme of the fundamentalist cults appear but a few steps from the depravity of Jonestown and Waco, where similar tactics were used.

Even mainstream Mormons are still instructed from childhood to avoid any source of information about their religion not sanctioned by the Church. All students of the faith are educated in a manner which introduces it's more bizarre doctrines only at a pace matched by their level of engagement and commitment. They are taught not to explore the conflicts which naturally arise when they are exposed to education in history or the sciences. Techniques of mental discipline are emphasized which direct the faithful to ignore doubts about the Church and in all cases to maintain faith in the teachings of the Prophet as the answer to all problems.

In this condition, mere teenagers are sent around the world as missionaries for a religion whose foundations, history and teachings they understand but little. Not surprisingly, when inevitable crises of faith occur, the results can be quite devastating.

One need only imagine confronting the realities of adult life in this state - knowing that to reject the faith is to face the certain loss of family, friends and economic security - to understand the psychological bind in which such persons find themselves. It is not surprising then how difficult it is for those indoctrinated to find their way out, and that this faith continues to be passed on to new converts and new generations despite what outsiders recognize to be its preposterous teachings.

THE NEW RELIGIONS

Since time immemorial there have been those who sought to salvage something of value from the complex, conflicting and often deeply troubling contents of the Bible. Some, including the alchemists and kabbalists, sought clues to secret knowledge they believed must be encoded in symbolic language within its passages. Others gave up on the scriptures and looked for new formulas to reconcile or integrate the reality of Nature with the imagined realm of spirits, angels, heaven and hell. As a class, these were the theosophists, and their most advanced visionary was an early scientist and Christian mystic named Emmanuel Swedenborg.

In some ways an early forerunner of the (post-disappointment) Millerites, Swedenborg believed that Judgment Day had already come to pass unnoticed, and that God had explained this to him directly. His description of Heaven was remarkably similar to - some say adopted as - the ideas of Joseph Smith. Unlike Smith, however, the man appears by all accounts to have been entirely sincere, and made no effort to found a sect or make money from the revelations he believed he received from God.

Apart from a small effect on the Mormons, Swedenborg's theology seems to have had little impact in the United States until after the millennial enthusiasms had passed. At that point they seem to have become popular with some who were looking for the next new religion, as well as with Universalists and other progressives whose social attitudes had brought them into conflict with mainstream religionists still resisting the abolition of slavery and the extension of equal rights to women. His ideas enjoyed a brief period of approval in the Burned Over District, as well as other parts of New York and New England until their adherents were overtaken by a new religion which resulted from a childhood prank played by two young Rochester girls.

These were the Fox sisters, who at the age of 11 and 15 respectively, discovered they could make surprisingly loud sounds by working the joints in their feet. This they did at first to annoy and mystify the members of their immediate family, until coming upon the idea to claim the knocking sounds were signs given by a ghost who lived in the house into which their family had recently moved. Thus was born the Spiritualist movement, which, despite the rapid uncovering of the girls' trickery, has persisted for over a century and has helped to create some of the more absurd ideas which continue into the New Age religions of the present.

Once the notion of direct contact with disembodied spirits was popularized, all manner of mediums and spirit guides came forth. Some of these were no doubt sincerely unable to distinguish the outpourings of their own subconscious minds from messages being sent by God, ghosts, and other imagined ethereal communicators. The technique of "spirit channeling" rapidly evolved, and has continued into the present, if the origin of the still-popular *A Course in Miracles* is correctly understood.[37] Needless to say, many charlatans also came forth, selling lies to anxious and gullible patrons. And while the tricks and techniques of these performers are well known and easily explained, there appears no end to the line of wishful believers.

A new chapter in this long, sad tale began in 1875, when Helena Blavatsky founded the Theosophical Society in New York City. The material concepts and spiritual notions upon which this group relied are so unique – embracing an occult view which incorporates several new classes of supernatural spirits and "elemental beings" - as to make them stand out even among those of the most imaginative of 19th century mystical thinkers.

After splitting into factions, Blavatsky's branch of the Society ultimately relocated to India, seeking to integrate Eastern philosophies with progressive values and their unique cosmology. There they achieved little of lasting impact beyond their "discovery" of a young boy, Jiddu Krishnamurti, living next door to their headquarters. The group believed Krishnamurti would be a great spiritual master, and supported his development in this direction. He did become a traveling preacher, though in adulthood he abandoned the group.

Madame Blavatsky's other lasting contributions to the world of the absurd include her belief in ancient wisdom mysteriously received from the mythical lost continent of Atlantis, and an imaginary set of non-physical records of all the world's past and future thought. These subsequently came to be known among merchants of the mystical and magical as the Akashic Records.

The Theosophical Society's European branch, under the leadership of Rudolph Steiner, differed with the Indian group over various ideological points. Though some elements of Steiner's philosophy appear quite bizarre, other aspects have been proved genuinely effective, whether or not divorced from mystical beliefs and rituals. He did, for example, make interesting contributions in the fields of agriculture and education, reflected in the principles of biointensive farming and the still-popular Waldorf Schools.

Those familiar with the history of Americans' fascination with Eastern and occult philosophies will see that most of the basic elements of today's New Age religions were in hand at the turn of the 20th century. As more Americans have become disillusioned with the antiquated structures and outdated dogma of the traditional religions, or alienated by their opposition to social progress, increasing numbers have turned to these stranger, but equally irrational ideas from which to adopt or fabricate religious beliefs.

Most Westerners are now accustomed to the practice of Hatha Yoga in their communities by people who do not hold to the polytheistic beliefs of the Hindus who developed it. Similarly the practice of various forms of meditation has become popular among persons who hold no particular religious views. That these practices were developed by believers in Buddhism or Hinduism appears today of little consequence. Some question if Buddhism should even be thought of as a religion, and it is clear that far fewer Westerners take seriously the absurdities of the Hindu Trinity than those of the Christian variety.

It might almost be said the influence of the Eastern religions is benign in the West, and perhaps brings benefits with the healthful practices of diet, exercise and meditation they promote. Clearly, any such benefits are derived from the practices themselves, independent of religious or mystical interpretations which may be attached by the practitioner. In fact, were it not for these attachments, the practices themselves are to be highly recommended.

Frequently, however, the disconnection is not made, and therein lies the problem. It is common to find among the modern successors to Madame Blavatsky a complex mix of religious and quasi-religious beliefs, often blended into a virtually incomprehensible soup of supernatural doctrines and myths.

NEW AGE RELIGION

The so-called New Age spirituality incorporates elements of the Eastern religions, theosophy, and the appropriation of often poorly understood Native American traditions, sometimes supplemented by teachings supposed to have come from disembodied entities living in this and other worlds. New Age believers share a willingness to replace reason with mysticism, and as a consequence remain vulnerable to a great wasting of their energies and to exploitation by a variety of charlatans in the endless search for signs and wonders.

New Age gurus promote a strange type of magical thinking, frequently incorporating notions of individual power to alter the future at will, a rejection of scientific realism and suspicion of all conventional bases of authority, however legitimate. These teachings so degrade the powers of critical reasoning those who receive them are often passionate advocates for the most outrageous of conspiracy theories.

As there are far too many variations on this theme to catalog them all, I shall instead attempt to briefly point out the key features of New Age thinking, and to show how their teaching is detrimental to believers and to society at large. In almost every case, the dangers are the same as those presented by the traditional churches, except that instead of encouraging violence and submission to authority, the New Age religions tend as strongly to teach against science, but toward confusion about, and retirement from effective participation in public affairs.

Subjectivity

Focus on an inner world of sensation, sometimes supplemented by the use of drugs which directly affect the nervous system, is a doorway to mysticism and a path to disengagement from the real world. If one abandons belief in objective truth, there is no way to correctly assess value, morality, or what actions are needed to advance one's own rights or the rights of others. Judging Truth solely, or even primarily by the extent to which a proposition *feels* true is a certain path to error, and a pattern sure to be exploited by unscrupulous manipulators.

Magical Thinking

Virtually all churches promote belief in magical powers to alter the natural world. In traditional religions these powers are typically assigned to the Almighty, and in some cases to saints, angels, or other special messengers who in one way or another can be petitioned to grant special favors to the faithful (a process frequently aided by the giving of money to some kind of priest). It is common, for example for Christians to be taught to pray to God or Jesus to give them things they want, despite the explicit instruction attributed to Jesus in Matthew this should not be done, and despite the easily-made observation and clear research evidence that praying for God's intercession (for example in the health of a sick person) has no effect on the material world.

New Age gurus instruct their followers to substitute themselves for the deity in their magical thinking, teaching one can *manifest* what one wants simply by holding an *intention* it be so, and that nature will conform to the will of the believer in ways she would not otherwise have done. This notion goes far beyond the concept of Positive Thinking, or a strategy for correcting one's own efforts toward constructive goal attainment. What is taught - and apparently believed by many - is the demonstrably destructive notion that simply wishing for something can literally make it so. While the absurdity of this notion will be obvious to most readers, all may not be familiar with the cleverness used to promote this belief, almost always as a strategy for selling books or "training" by some kind of mystic teacher.[38]

Constant Healing

In place of the earlier promises of Redemption and Salvation, New Age thinkers are frequently engaged in perpetual efforts at healing - of them-selves, others, or the entire planet. Modern charlatans teach foundationless theories involving electromagnetic frequencies, selling magic crystals and offering various forms of readings and "energy healing" to a seemingly endless train of traumatized customers and prospective successors willing to pay for their services and instruction.

Behind the Skirts of Science

As most persons in developed countries have become familiar with the success of the scientific method in unlocking ancient mysteries, the merchants of superstition now trail behind, frequently claiming scientists share their beliefs, or that their doctrines are supported or soon will be by "emerging science." These claims are to some degree popular among all religionists who seek to bolster the foundations of superstition, and particularly among those who promote New Age ideas.

It should be noted here that, in truth, most scientists do not profess supernatural beliefs. In fact, only a minority believe in a God who influences worldly events and but seven percent of the American Academy of Sciences believe in a God who answers prayers. If there is comfort to be found by religionists in the actual facts of this case, they are welcome to it.

Typical of the New Age gurus is the claim that fantasied mind control over the material world is in some way related to the principles of quantum physics. This misrepresentation of science and misuse of scientific sounding language - which physicist Murray Gell-Mann labeled "Quantum Flapdoodle" - so distorts the actual findings of science as to render them nonsensical, and appears to have appeal in direct proportion to the believers' ignorance of the principles involved.

On the rare occasion one of the purveyors of this pseudo-scientific nonsense comes up against a real scientist, the results can be quite different from the confident pretense of authority typically portrayed in their books and lectures. An amusing video on YouTube[39] shows the result when evolutionary biologist Richard Dawkins confronts New Age guru Deepak Chopra on his use of the term "Quantum Healing" in which the visibly shaken Dr. Chopra asserts he uses the term only as a metaphor, and does not mean to imply what he has clearly and deliberately misled legions of his followers to believe. More commonly, the proper disposition of scientists to be judicious in their statements creates what Sam Harris has called an unlovely asymmetry in which, while true scientists speak with care and qualification, "one often finds people with no scientific training speaking with apparent certainty about the theological significance of quantum mechanics, cosmology, or molecular biology."

A similar process can be seen at work in the writings of a depressed alcoholic brain surgeon named Eben Alexander who contracted a rare and nearly fatal brain infection at a time when, by his own admission, his career was in steep decline. While in a coma, and for days after, Alexander experienced several vivid hallucinations, a fact he also concedes. However, Alexander maintains the most real-seeming of his visions - that he was taken by an attractive young woman for a ride on a giant butterfly to meet Jesus - actually happened, arguing like many New Agers (and all evidence to the contrary) that his consciousness resides outside of, and functions independently of his brain.

Though, perhaps for the better, Alexander has not returned to the practice of medicine, in his best-selling book[40] and personal appearances he claims credibility for his story based on his former practice as a brain surgeon, citing several arguments that sound persuasively scientific to the common person. Perhaps it is needless to say Alexander's claims are dismissed utterly by the very physicians who treated him, as well as by independent experts in the neurosciences.

Though claims of scientific support and use of scientific-sounding language are commonly used to prop up the fantastic notions of New Age gurus and booksellers, when it is shown where evidence established through scientific methods refutes their claims, the position rapidly shifts. Then science is just another religion: rigid, reductionist, and confined to a limiting system of constraints that hides the spiritual truth knowable only through subjective experience. It would be better for such mental gymnasts to hold to one or the other position, if only to limit the number of ways in which they can be shown to be mistaken.

CHAPTER V

THE IMMORALITY OF RELIGIOUS INDOCTRINTION

I HAVE shown the great harm inflicted upon the progress of civilization by belief in sacred texts, supernatural causes, and the doctrines which flow from them, and by the techniques used to perpetuate acceptance of such doctrines against the natural objections of conscience and reason. Here I address in detail the most powerful and insidious of those techniques, that being the indoctrination of children with supernatural beliefs.

Knowing their teachings to be without rational foundation, churches demand access to the minds of children at an age when they are powerless to refuse, and lack the intellectual capacity to challenge the credibility of religious myth and dogma. That this is permitted to continue is a great shame upon our society, calling into doubt the depth of our commitment to human rights and perpetuating into future generations an ignorance of nature and a weakness of mind detrimental to society as a whole.

I present below six points which in their totality show the immorality of indoctrinating children with supernatural beliefs and why all who wish to see society progress must demand an end to this practice.

Terrorizing and Exploiting Children

Among the greatest harms resulting from religious indoctrination is the damage done to the minds of young children. In Christian churches children are taught they are under constant surveillance by dead relatives and other invisible creatures, all agents of a fierce and judgmental god who knows their secret thoughts and plans brutal punishment for any deviation from the demands of the church, however natural and irresistible their thoughts and impulses might be.

So horrible are the effects of these teachings that most adults rapidly learn to discount and forget their terrifying effect on the childish mind. Yet but a moment's reflection on the world of spirits, demons and eternal punishment which is laid before the impressionable minds of children must cause any thoughtful person to shudder with disgust. A moment's additional reflection will reveal how even as adults the victims of this indoctrination remain affected – not for the better - in their most private thoughts and most intimate acts.

Of greatest concern is the teaching of a religiously-based moral code which treats children's natural sexual development as sinful, deviant and deserving of punishment. It would be impossible to measure the psychological effects of such ideas, much less the social impact of institutionalized sexual repression. One need only consider how many lives are ruined through family and societal rejection of young people who do not conform to heterosexual norms to begin to appreciate the extent of the damage done by religious indoctrination. Add to this the emotional difficulties, disease, unplanned pregnancies and attendant economic problems which result when religious meddlers obstruct the proper education of children about sex and reproduction. Add again the antiquated social attitudes which are perpetuated regarding sex roles and sexuality leaving both children and adults hobbled by inhibition, vulnerable to oppression, and conditioned to tolerate and repeat abuse.

Finally, consider the obvious danger when religious teachers who are themselves the victims of such unwholesome influences are given power over, and unsupervised access to children taught to obey church authorities under threat of punishment. Decades of revelations of clergy scandals, and the clear signs of more on the way, should remove any doubt how great and widespread is this danger.

Less widely known are the monstrous practices engaged in by Mormons at least into the 1970s, in which teenagers were coerced into submitting to conditioning experiments reminiscent of "A Clockwork Orange" in which attempts were made to "cure" them of their Same Sex Attraction by administering chemical emetics and electrical shocks to their genitals. Mormons and some other Christian groups continue to this day to attempt conversion of homosexuals into heterosexuals through a variety of similarly absurd and inhumane strategies.

Teaching Against Science

I have established above the extent to which churches and other religious institutions have actively suppressed the progress of science, both on their own and in concert with allied states. While the worst part of the Christian Dark Ages is past - scientists are no longer prosecuted for heresy and sedition in Western countries - blasphemy remains a crime in some Islamic states. Even in the United States, efforts continue to promote the teaching of the Christian creation myth, and the slightly more subtle concept of Intelligent Design, as competing theories of nature in the science classes of our public schools.

While it was once reasonable to think the complexity of nature demanded an intelligent Creator (I argued this belief in the earlier Parts of this work) hundreds of years of scientific progress have shown this notion to be without foundation. Yet religious zealots continue in their efforts to confuse adults and miseducate children regarding the origin of the universe and of species on Earth. It is consequently not surprising that Americans trail in their understanding of these things compared to those educated in other developed countries.

While many conservative Christians recognize the absurdity of teaching the 17th century theory the world was created a mere six thousand years ago, this very notion, along with denial of evolution and geological science is still taught in private religious institutions. Newer religions teach of *elemental beings*, immortal spirits and magic powers, sometimes obfuscated with claims of scientific foundation. All of these notions are outside the observable reality of nature, and teaching them serves to confuse, if not to intentionally undermine public understanding of science and nature.

Promoting Gullibility and Passivity

I have previously noted the extent to which most churches have made peace and partnerships with tyranny. The enslavement, theft of resources and shocking abuses carried out during the age of European colonialism rarely did much to offend the churches of Rome or of England, both of which happily supported monarchs and their "democratic" successors in endless violations of every human right and principle of decency.

Teaching the people to accept the so-called *Divine Right of Kings* was long the stock in trade of the Christian churches. In more recent times they have continued to support the power structure of all nations where their position of privilege might be maintained, and have smiled upon all manner of oppression and resistance to revolutionary change, urging the faithful to submit to the authority of their oppressors.

Just as the Roman church was used by Spain as a tool of enslavement, successor oligarchs and dictators throughout Latin America have maintained the privileged position of the church in return for its continued support of their oppression, exploitation and abuse of the people. Even when it's own Archbishop was murdered at the altar in El Salvador and its nuns were raped and killed, the Roman Catholic hierarchy continued to castigate local clergy who spoke out on behalf of the rights of the people.

How then does religion so effectively support the oppression, robbery and murder of the people? By continuing to teach against critical thinking, by persuading the faithful to ignore their common sense and the protests of conscience, and teaching them to follow instead the directions of priests and generals. While each has its unique emphasis - the mainstream

Christians promising their traditional heaven while the Mormons promise their faithful men an afterlife of polygamy and godlike planetary rule; the Muslims promising even more voluptuous virgins than the Mormons - all teach that submission to authority in this life, sometimes to the point of murder and suicide, will be rewarded in the next.

Instead of teaching children to think for themselves, and how to detect the work of charlatans, parents in all cultures continue to turn over the moral education of their children to those who have the most to fear from strong, intelligent minds. By teaching children to trust in the authority of others, to deny their own doubts and to suppress conscience and reason in favor of dogma, churches sow confusion and train children in mental weakness and submissiveness, leaving them easy targets for oppression. Not surprisingly, the young of all religions remain the pawns of child molesters, exploiters and warmongers.

Fostering Hatred and Discrimination

All churches claim to teach love, and in so doing all but a few prove themselves false. In all of the organized religions, children are taught to believe they belong to a special group, and are different from and (with varying degrees of subtlety) superior to their peers. They are taught they must hold certain beliefs, and that those who do not will rightly be made to suffer in this life and be tortured or abandoned in the hereafter.

It is but a short leap from believing that infidels deserve punishment to believing it is just and proper to see to the task. This is manifested in innumerable ways, from social shunning and economic favoritism to supporting unjust and discriminatory laws; even to supporting violence and conducting warfare based on religious differences.

Faithful Christians are called upon by church authorities to become actively involved in political efforts to deny civil rights and benefits to those who do not share their beliefs. The Catholic church, in combination with other conservative Christian groups, has had stunning success in limiting even Constitutionally protected rights - such as that of a woman to prevent or abort pregnancy - when the free exercise of these rights conflicts with church doctrine. These groups have joined with other Christian churches to oppose the protection and free exercise of equal rights by persons whose sexual orientation or practices conflict with church teaching, fighting state by state battles to deny civil marriage and other benefits to fellow citizens whose sexuality fails to meet with church approval.

It is not hard to see how the teaching of group chauvinism and the promotion of discrimination of various sorts sometimes leads to overt hatred and violence. Just as the Christian churches defended institutional slavery and racial discrimination for centuries, justifying unspeakable acts of inhumanity in the minds of their perpetrators, so has the churches' opposition to sexual freedom given rise to brutality and murder. The deaths of physicians Barnett Slepian and George Miller, among many others, must be seen first and foremost as the result of their killers' adoption of religious ideas which begin with the teachings of conservative Christians.

Justifying War and Exploitation

Having endorsed Monarchy and the enslavement of Africans, the evolution of Christian support for the enslavement and colonization of other people, continuing into the mid-twentieth century, was not surprising. Nor was the evolution of colonial oppression into wars of liberation, and the resulting conflict between capitalist and socialist economic systems.

It should be even less a surprise that an officially Jewish nation formed on territory populated primarily by Muslims has led to a century of growing violence in the Middle East, or that the echo of Christian wars of religious conquest still resound throughout the world. Neither is it possible for even a casual observer to overlook the role played by factions within Islam, and their official State sponsors, in perpetuating conflict throughout the region. Here the manipulations of the so-called Islamic Republics compete for blame with the barbarity of Israeli treatment of Palestinian Arabs and the intrigues of the nominally Christian nations. Still all sides use religion to inflame and mobilize partisans against one another, each faction teaching its children their cause alone is endorsed by God.

Denial of Religious Freedom

As the religious indoctrination of children remains a near-universal phenomenon it may at first seem strange to argue its universal recognition as a crime. Yet two existing international treaties relating to this point, the most widely shared statements of human rights ever known, clearly spell out the right of all persons to be free of coercion in religious matters, and the recognition this right extends to children as well as adults.

The Universal Declaration of Human Rights (1948) states in its Eighteenth Article: *Everyone has the right to freedom of thought, conscience and religion; this right includes freedom to change his religion or belief, and freedom, either alone or in community with others and in public or private, to manifest his religion or belief in teaching, practice, worship and observance.*

The United Nations Convention on the Rights of the Child (1989) states in its Fourteenth Article: *1. States Parties shall respect the right of the child to freedom of thought, conscience and religion. 2. States Parties shall respect the rights and duties of the parents and, when applicable, legal guardians, to provide direction to the child in the exercise of his or her right in a manner consistent with the evolving capacities of the child. 3. Freedom to manifest one's religion or beliefs may be subject only to such limitations as are prescribed by law and are necessary to protect public safety, order, health or morals, or the fundamental rights and freedoms of others.*

If, as shown above, the legal right to religious freedom is protected in children as well as adults, and if the rights of parents to direct a child's religious practices are limited to those consistent with the child's capacities and only those other limits as apply to all persons, then all religious indoctrination should be held suspect. If a person has any religious freedom at all, it must include the freedom to refuse indoctrination into the beliefs of another, and to be free of coercion of any kind in the decision to accept or reject religious instruction.

As it cannot properly be said parents have the right to indoctrinate children in beliefs the child cannot fully comprehend, it is proper they should refrain from any religious instruction while the child lacks the capacity to fully evaluate the credibility of its lessons. To hold otherwise opens the door to all manner of abuse of persons with acknowledged limitation of intellectual functioning and renders any concept of religious freedom effectively without meaning.

Yet, everywhere we see the opposite. Parents believe themselves to be doing good by subjecting their children to rituals which they cannot grasp - sometimes merely boring or frightening, and sometimes involving their physical mutilation - and a form of moral instruction which often fills the imagination with a long list of sins not yet known of or considered. This sorry state of affairs will continue until the teaching of supernatural fables and myths as truth is universally recognized as abusive to children and harmful to society. A simple corrective comes to mind: instead of presuming to tell children what religious beliefs they have, let us instead wait until they are adults, and ask them.

Those who would secure the liberty of generations to come must demand the United States Senate cease its long and embarrassing delay, and ratify the United Nations Convention on the Rights of the Child. This should be implemented by an Act which clearly states the rights of children to be protected from any form of religious or political indoctrination, and should include a statement substantially as follows:

Children are entitled to be protected by the law in all of their rights, equally as are adults. All children have the right to freedom of thought, and to be free from indoctrination or coercion in the development of their social, political and religious values and beliefs. Children have the right to be free of religious or political bias in their education, to refuse any education intended to influence their political or religious beliefs, and to refuse participation in any political activity or religious ritual.

Those responsible for the education of children have the obligation to inform them of these rights, and to assist them in their protection. Interference in the political and religious freedom of children should be treated as an act of abuse, subject to the same civil procedures for reporting, investigation and adjudication by the authorities as apply to any other form of child abuse or neglect.

CHAPTER VI

CHURCH AND STATE IN THE NEW MILLENNIUM

TO CORRECTLY assess the current state of religious affairs in America, we must examine not only how society treats those within the mainstream of the dominant culture, but also its treatment of those who live in some manner or degree outside it; and secondly the extent to which churches confine themselves to private conduct, as opposed to interfering in the rights of others or in the machinery of civil government. On these scores a fair assessment will hold the churches a continuing danger. To observe that Christians and Jews in America for the most part now treat each other with civility does not exonerate the charge.

In America and much of Europe, Islam has replaced Judaism as the principal target of religious bigots, and the frontiers of religious belief are now occupied by those who wish at the least to be free of coercion in matters of conscience, and to be free, should it seem to them best, to reject religion entirely. The limits of religious freedom are therefor not to be found in the extent to which Christians and Jews may exercise their rights, but rather the extent to which those of Muslims, atheists, agnostics and other less populous groups are held secure. Thus, placing a menorah next to the creche in the town square does not diminish the offense to Constitutional rights so much as to multiply the perpetrators.

While serious challenges are faced by American believers in Islam, it is the right of nonbelievers to be free from coercion and the misuse of governmental powers which remains under greatest attack. So unbalanced is this struggle, that at the slightest resistance to their domination of civic affairs it is common to hear religious zealots complain of a loss of their own rights. This is their perception when denied the opportunity to promote their doctrines at the expense of others, in the public schools and in the public square.[41]

For many Americans, most especially those who occupy a place outside the cultural mainstream, churches remain a constant enemy. The self-appointed guardians of community morality continue to argue that their own values and customs should be adopted and enforced by government, and that all must obey. Personal sexual behavior, private medical decisions and regulation of civil marriage are all current areas of legal dispute where religious organizations and individuals have banded together to extend their power not only over their own adherents, but also over fellow citizens who hold to other, or to no religious beliefs.

Here then is our great challenge: to protect the Wall of Separation between Church and State enshrined in our Constitution, and to assure that in every way the machinery of government operates in response to human interests, denying to religious doctrine any role in its weighing of rights and values.

Our political system remains dangerously susceptible to religious manipulation, and in this the American people are their own enemy. By lending credence to the claim of a supernatural basis to morality, they still overwhelmingly prefer candidates for public office who profess strong religious beliefs. Knowing this, American politicians from the time of Jefferson have struggled to appear pious to the voters, even when they were not.

Stateless Christian Fundamentalism

Sadly, Americans' tolerance of religious manipulators has led to more than the sacking of bank accounts by Rolex-wearing televangelists and efforts to bankrupt Planned Parenthood. Religious freedom is constantly challenged by those who seek to compel prayer in public schools (despite the reported direction of Jesus to pray in private[42]), to introduce religious "theories" into the teaching of science, to deny their neighbors access to modern means of birth control and pregnancy termination, and to deny equal rights to fellow citizens based on their disapproval of their neighbors' sexuality.

Catholics argue to be exempted from laws governing all employers, and other religious conservatives up the ante by proposing legislation to allow businesses to refuse service to those who do not share their owners' religious beliefs. Religious opponents of abortion rights have publicly harassed and stalked physicians who provide legal health services to women, resulting in bombings of clinics and assassinations of physicians and other clinic staff. Well-heeled Christian extremists, following a decades-long strategy of secrecy and manipulation have helped to shape not only the political landscape of America, but have also extended their reach internationally, sometimes with lethal con-sequences.

Most Americans are familiar with the obligatory annual ritual of the President's attendance at the so-called National Prayer Breakfast in Washington. Few however know much if anything about the highly secretive organization which sponsors this event. This group, charmingly known among its members and friends as The Family[43] has for decades cultivated a particular strain of Christian fundamentalism, providing housing, support and contacts for conservative religious politicians in Washington and those who wish to know them.

Pursuing its "Key Man" strategy, this group has spread its influence to national leaders around the world, and particularly in Africa, fueling rampant discrimination on that continent against persons who do not display a Christian fundamentalist-approved flavor of sexual expression. In some countries this and other officially stateless Christian organizations, supplemented by the efforts of church-based evangelists, rival the threat which continues to be presented by state-sponsored religions. In so doing they hamper progress toward separation of Church and State around the world.

Stateless Islamic Fundamentalism

There are few examples of the foolishness of marrying reli-gion with politics that rival the disastrous consequences of America's Cold War effort to undermine Soviet control of Afghanistan. Seeing an opportunity to exploit the religiously-motivated Muslim *Mujahedin*, America provided military and other material support to a group of Islamic extremists who indeed succeeded in driving the Soviets out of Afghanistan, allowing in their place the rise of the Taliban, and creating a friendly host country from which these same extremists began to attack America's own interests.

Over the intervening years al Qaeda evolved into a network which has brought increased sophistication and technology to terrorists around the world, connected to no national government and committed only to the making of holy war against America and other perceived enemies. No one should need to be reminded of the devastation which has been visited on cities in America and around the globe as a result of this fatal mistake.

This is not to say the threat presented by Islamic Funda-mentalism arises only from America's misguided foreign policy in Afghanistan. The world's tolerance - largely at America's insistence - of the decades of humiliation forced upon the Arab populations of Palestine has brewed a dangerous mix of religious hatred and violence. This is fueled daily by new acts of illegal colonization carried out by Israel on behalf of its Jewish population, most of whom are imported into the region from other countries around the world. For decades the desperate cries of Palestinian refugees - driven into camps when the nation of Israel was carved out of their homeland – have been ignored, their suffering treated as so much collateral damage in the global reaction to Nazi atroci-ties.

By playing into the hands of Jewish extremists in Israel and their politically active American supporters, our nation has lent fuel to the fire of Muslim resentment, and provided a painful example of what appears to be our officially nonreligious nation siding with the adherents of one faith against those of another in a brutal taking of land and resources.

Israel and the Islamic Republics

Whether the genie of violent Islamic Fundamentalism can be put back into the bottle is, in the early years of the 21st century, a question one hesitates to ask. For America's part, we can reasonably expect no progress, and therefore no peace on this front, as long as we give legitimacy to claims of religious hegemony, or accept military and political actions justified by the demands of a state religion.

To assume a position of moral leadership America must press on all fronts for the assurance of equal human rights for all, and should be refusing military aid to any State - Christian, Jewish or Muslim - which denies equal rights to any of its people. Even these actions are unlikely to be enough, unless America and the other nations of the world are willing to demand adherence by all states to the international laws which all have endorsed.

Sensible as such a policy may be, and familiar as it may sound to those who recall the Presidency of James E. Carter, the adoption of such a policy is virtually impossible to achieve at the present time. Under the influence of foreign lobbyists and their American kin, our country continues to protect the colonial policies of Israel, crushing the hopes and aspirations of the Arab world in the process.

Emboldened by our protection even for its most obvious crimes against humanity, Israel has demanded America surrender a convicted Israeli spy - before even his minimum sentence has been served - and demands Palestinians surrender forever their expectation of equal rights and that they forever accept the governance of a Jewish Religious State over the very homes in which they once lived. Unless these demands are met, Israeli political leaders insist they will continue to oppress and colonize their neighbors without regard to international law or principles of human decency.

Our country has recently borne the humiliation of needing to be reminded by South African Archbishop Desmond Tutu[44] of our duty to support the rights of the oppressed, and to protect Freedom of Speech in our own country. This, when he spoke out in support of those working peacefully to end Israeli oppression in occupied Palestine by promoting boycotts, disinvestment and sanctions (BDS) - the same tactics which freed South Africa from racist apartheid. He felt compelled to do so because of policies affecting who is permitted to speak on American college campuses and the actions of American politicians in response to Israeli propaganda against the BDS campaign. That our country needs to be reminded in this way of its own core values should be the cause of deep reflection by all Americans.

It is not to Israel alone that America has surrendered its honor. Other undemocratic governments are treated by our country with equal deference because Americans remain overly dependent on the oil produced by Arab states, and it has long been our practice to suffer or perpetrate upon others any injustice in order to maintain our wasteful profit-driven energy policies. In countries where women are denied even the right to drive automobiles, where atheism is outlawed and journalists are sentenced to floggings and long prison terms for "insulting Islam" American military and political support remains on display.

A great and desperately needed change could be made in the world were America to take the position that religion has no more place in the governance of other countries than it has in our own, and that we will no longer support nations which claim the right, based on an official religion, to abuse their own citizens or those of neighboring countries. America could once again lead the world by proclaiming no religion is entitled to our diplomatic recognition,[45] much less its own country and its own nuclear arsenal.

Religion and Politics in "Christian" America

America began the new millennium with what Jefferson called the Wall of Separation between Church and State effectively under siege by conservative Christians and their allies in government. In 1993 televangelist Pat Robertson had declared "They have kept us in submission because they have talked about separation of church and state. There is no such thing in the Constitution. It's a lie of the Left, and we're not going to take it anymore." This following an opinion by Chief Justice William Rehnquist (in which he was outvoted) which held "The 'wall of separation between church and State' is a metaphor based on bad history, a metaphor which has proved useless as a guide to judging. It should be frankly and explicitly abandoned."

Though in this opinion Mr. Justice Rehnquist was in the minority on the Court, his views have continued to pervade its rulings to the present time. Just this year the sharply divided Court ruled in a five to four decision that the opening of governmental meetings with Christian prayers was Constitutional because it was "part of our Nation's fabric."

This state of affairs has evolved in large part from a series of political moves in which wealthy conservatives, seeing their policies unattractive to most Americans, formed coalitions first with former Dixiecrats of the racist South, and subsequently with their new allies' religious brethren throughout the country. Thus in the 1960s the Republican Party ceased to be a voice for moderate business leaders and continued the march toward political and religious extremism which began during the height of the Cold War, and now characterizes its domestic policies and electoral strategies - a far cry from its origin as the party of Sumner and Lincoln.

Since the end of the Second World War, American foreign policy has constantly used Religion as a tool for identifying enemies and mobilizing popular support against them. Shortly after overthrowing the elected governments of Guatemala and Iran, President Dwight D. Eisenhower proposed, and later signed a law changing our nation's long standing but unofficial motto *E Pluribus Unum* (From Many, One), proclaiming in its stead *In God We Trust*. At the same time the official language of the Pledge of Allegiance to the American Flag was changed to insert the words "under God." This reflected an ongoing campaign to use religion to mobilize political support for Cold War policies and actions which we now see to have been against the interest of our nation and the principles for which it stands.

This strategy has continued in the intervening years, reflected in American support for the overthrow of elected governments, opposition to popular revolutions and support for dictatorships throughout Latin America and in the Middle East. In varying ways the Christian churches have contributed to this strategy, as has an organized community of Jewish supporters of Israel. The predictable result has been to nurture intractable resentments against our country in our own hemisphere and throughout the Muslim world.

Domestically, we see continuing challenges by churches to our Constitution and to the rights of those who do not share their beliefs. These incorporate the aforementioned insistence their doctrines be imposed in the public schools through efforts to promote public praying and the teaching of religious creation myths in the place of Science. Still we see examples of Christian religious doctrine brazenly taught in some public schools, decades after all such actions have been explicitly prohibited.[46] In recent years this has been extended to advocating for school voucher programs designed to bring public tax dollars into religious schools which are otherwise ineligible to receive them.

The Christian preoccupation with sex and reproduction persists unabated, growing from ancient concepts about procreation which were never accepted by the common people, and from the unwholesome control of church institutions by men schooled in the subjugation of natural desires (and of women). In this we see frequent examples of what psychologists call *reaction formation,* when that which is denied in oneself is externalized and demonized, either in its imagined cause or object. Thus we understand fantasies of Satanic temptation and the obsession with suppressing the sexuality of women and girls - from absurdities like Father-Daughter Purity Dances and burkas to the monstrous practice of female genital mutilation. So too are we enlightened about the ravings of male preachers who, at the same time they are later found to have been patronizing prostitutes of both sexes, rail against the very acts which they desire and perform in secret.

We see here also yet another complexity of the Christian mind, wherein children are proclaimed to be gifts from God, whereas the burden of others' unwanted pregnancy is treated as the wages of sin, with all manner of efforts made to assure these pregnancies occur, and nothing be permitted to interfere with their progress.

The integration of Christian conservatives and their wealthy, self-interested allies in the current formation of the Republican Party makes for strange bedfellows. Here the followers of Jesus are led to fight for government policies - including unfair tax structures, deregulation of dangerous industries and elimination of public programs to help the economically disadvantaged - which serve only to increase the suffering of the poor and to advance the interests of those once considered as unlikely to achieve salvation as a camel passing through the eye of a needle. But what do Christians gain in return for abandoning the teachings of their Christ? Here they would be well advised to respect the adage of being careful what one prays for.

In successfully demanding sex education be restricted to unrealistic church-sanctioned approaches, such as Abstinence-Only education and Purity Pledges, Christian advocates have succeeded in *increasing* unplanned pregnancies and the inci- dence of sexually transmitted diseases in America and around the world. Further, it has been shown that teenagers adjust to such indoctrination by increasing their experimentation with anal and oral sex, likely not what the sponsors had in mind.

Similarly, the social strategies designed to ignore the suffering of the poor and to limit access to birth control have been shown to increase the likelihood unplanned pregnancies will be intentionally aborted. And while claims that "welfare programs hurt the poor" may provide a convenient cover for racial and other resentments, and help free the wealthy from their civic obligations, both the churches and their monied allies are happy to share in government largesse with special tax breaks, wasteful government contracts, and so-called Faith Based Initiatives designed to provide tax dollar support for religious organizations.

I pause on the subject of Faith Based Initiatives to take note of some recent political developments. When this concept of intentionally funneling public resources into Christian churches was first openly proposed by President George W. Bush, it was immediately - and properly - rejected by the Congress. President Bush proceeded to implement his initiative through Executive Order, funneling two billion dollars a year[47] into churches and their service activities, and specifically exempting the recipients of these funds from the requirement that government contractors not discriminate in employment on the basis of religion.

When President Barack H. Obama reviewed these policies in 2011, his staff was told that interfering with the nearly-decade long practice of religious employment discrimination would significantly disrupt import-ant community services. Characteristically seeking to deny ammunition to his Conservative critics, President Obama retained the discrimination exemption, leaving taxpayers and job seekers deprived of the government's protection of their First Amendment rights.

Proceeding then with the Christian obsession with procreation, we have seen efforts not only to prevent sex education and access to contraception, but even more absurd intrusions of religious beliefs into public policies, such as President George W. Bush's interference in the conduct of fetal stem cell research, and more aggressive, sometimes lethal attacks on the right of women to voluntarily terminate pregnancy, a right which has been upheld by the Supreme Court for over forty years.

Most will be familiar with the legislative and other efforts made by Christian groups to interfere with women who wish to terminate a pregnancy, and with the medical professionals who provide abortion services. In recent years Planned Parenthood has come under vigorous attack, with efforts made in the Congress to deny to this organization and its community affiliates funding for any service, whether abortion-related or not.

Increasingly restrictive state laws have been passed, seeking to limit specific abortion procedures and pushing back the point in pregnancy beyond which abortions may not be legally performed. Burdensome regulatory requirements have been adopted, making it practically or financially impossible for clinics providing abortions to remain in operation. These have been matched with efforts to make the process of obtaining an abortion more difficult, time consuming and expensive, even to the point of intentionally humiliating patients. Legislators in several states have recently proposed laws to require women seeking abortions to submit to unnecessary vaginal probes, and to be shown ultrasound images of the fetuses they wish to abort.

It may be wondered why a political party structured primarily to protect the interests of wealthy businessmen cares to align itself with such a program. It is possible some of our country's business leaders genuinely share in the beliefs of their religiously-motivated allies. It can also be clearly seen the manipulation of religious conservatives is a crass political tactic in which abortion, like the perceived threat of equal rights for homosexuals, is turned into a "wedge" issue - intentionally dividing the religious from moderate candidates, and from the influence of their fellow citizens.

By placing discriminatory initiatives on the ballot, and by fielding electoral candidates sworn to even the most impossible agendas (such as a constitutional amendment to outlaw abortion) political strategists mobilize large numbers of religiously motivated voters and volunteers and vast pools of campaign contributions. These are then used to promote policies which greatly increase the suffering of the poor and which devastate the safety and natural environment of the average citizen, all for the profit of monied elites.

I proceed now to address the non-legislative, and often illegal abuses to which women seeking abortions, and those who serve them, are subjected.

Groups have created false family planning clinics to steer women away from genuine healthcare providers, offering free pregnancy testing followed by efforts to coerce their unwitting clients into carrying unwanted pregnancies to term. The presence of demonstrators outside clinics where abortions are actually performed have become a common sight. Frequently picketers harass women entering these facilities, to the point many such clinics now employ escorts to safely conduct their clients to their doors.

Incidents of disruption at abortion clinics, ranging from hate mail and harassing phone calls to physical blockades, reached historic highs during the years of the George W. Bush Presidency, never falling below 10,000 such incidents per year across the US and Canada.[48] During those years incidents of trespassing and clinic vandalism also peaked, reaching over 700 such incidents in 2005.

Some abortion opponents remain unsatisfied with these less violent tactics. Having argued themselves into the position that termination of a pregnancy is the equivalent of murder, some have adopted that tactic themselves. Since 1977 eight persons working at clinics providing abortions have been murdered by Christian extremists. During this same period there have been 17 attempted murders, 42 clinic bombings and 181 instances of arson. The effect of these attacks, as intended, has been to reduce the number of practitioners willing to perform abortions and to terrorize women seeking to exercise their legal rights.

Moving on to that other great wedge issue, I shall now briefly review the recent efforts of churches to deny equal rights on account of how their fellow citizens express them-selves sexually.

I have previously noted how fundamentalist Christians have promoted discrimination in other countries, even to the point of Uganda's contemplation of the death penalty for homosexual acts. And while violence and predation have long been a common experience of many gay people in America, here the public actions of the churches have been primarily focused on the denial of equal rights, most recently the right to marry and to provide military service to our country.

The absurdity of Americans needing to fight for the privilege of serving their country in uniform appears to be at last behind us. That such a long and expensive battle was necessary is an embarrassment to our country; the losses we have all sustained through rejecting the service of our fellow citizens, a tragedy. We can only celebrate the end of such foolishness. Sadly, we are not so advanced in the struggle for equal rights to enter the state-sanctioned marriage contract.

All countries recognize the importance of providing a kind of contract which allows two individuals to enter a life partnership, protecting the privileges and duties which attend such a relationship. Unlike business partnerships, the marriage contract attends to the most personal aspects of life: parenthood, inheritance, and even the right to be present with a sick or dying partner in hospital.

Having claimed religious significance for this relationship, and the concession for performing related ceremonial functions, churches seek not only to control their own rituals but also the civil arrangements pertaining to all persons. Here the churches appear to see they are also fighting a losing battle, but still the fight continues. Contrast with this embarrassing situation the way the issue is handled in Europe, where in effect there is no issue at all.

In Europe, couples who marry confirm the contract in the presence of a public official. If they also wish to ritualize the act with some sort of religious blessing, they do so as they choose. In America, the churches provide not only the religious ceremony but also act as agents of the state in officiating the execution of the legal contract. Having grown accustomed to acting in this way, and to applying their own standards as to who may be married where, they have arrogated to themselves the right to say who may marry at all. And so they have sought to deny marriage to couples of the same sex; not merely in their own places of business, but everywhere.

The 1996 Defense of Marriage Act was passed in Congress with veto-proof majorities and so, it is said, the bill was reluctantly signed into law by President William J. Clinton. This law denied federal recognition - for example in the awarding of benefits - to persons legally married in states which did not discriminate against same-sex couples, as state courts were then beginning to require. As more such cases were decided in favor of equality, churches moved to have laws passed, and in some cases sought amendments to state constitutions solely to deny the right to a state-sanctioned marriage contract to persons whose sexuality they for some reason find threatening. Perhaps the most famous such case was California Proposition 8, placed on the ballot by a coalition of religious organizations dominated by Catholics and Mormons.

The Church of Jesus Christ of Latter Day Saints actively raised funds from its members inside and outside of California to change that state's constitution after its own courts had ruled sex-based discrimination in marriage unconstitutional. While Catholic organizations and others did so to a lesser degree, an estimated 45% of out-of-state campaign funding and 80-90% of door to door volunteer labor in support of the proposition was supplied by Mormons.[49]

The fear-based campaign was successful, and the amendment promptly appealed to the courts. Neither the Governor nor the Attorney General of California was willing to defend the amendment in court, and it was struck down at both the District and Appellate levels. As the Supreme Court declined to hear the case, the amendment died when opportunities to appeal ran out, and Californians returned to marrying whom they chose.

The opponents of equal rights celebrated the Supreme Court's inaction, as it allows the state by state struggle against equality to continue. This, no doubt, is a boon to those who continue to use the issue to mobilize financial contributions and voter turnout in support of candidates whose loyalties are plainly not with the common people.

I have shown in this chapter the many ways in which the churches, seeing their powers waning, have struggled with ever greater vigor - and increasingly through attempts to manipulate the machinery of government - to maintain control over the lives of the people. I trust I have also shown the evil inherent in this behavior, and that it is both the right and duty of the American People to call it to its too long delayed end.

CHAPTER VII

CONCLUSIONS

Yitzak Rabin, Shannon Lowney, Rodney Dickens
Rachel Corrie, Abdulrahman Al-Awlaki, Malala Yousafzai

TO CONCLUDE this discussion and introduce my final thoughts, I have asked to be prepared an icon, as it were, to be contemplated by the reader. This is composed of six photographs of persons whose names and images should properly be known to all Americans. All are martyrs, in their way, to the religious beliefs of others, and each stands in the place of many others who have similarly suffered. Two are the victims of state violence, and four of attacks by non-state actors.

As of this writing, only one remains alive, and still lives under threat, having survived a gunshot to the head. Her name is Malala Yousafzai. She was 15 years old when attacked by the Pakistani Taliban for speaking publicly for the right of girls to be educated. Since her case is the most recent, and her brave young voice can still be heard, it is perhaps the most easily recalled.

Likely less well remembered - though certainly not forgotten - is Rachel Corrie, a 23 year old American citizen run over with a bulldozer by an Israeli soldier intent on demolishing the home of a Palestinian family in occupied Gaza. Less likely to be memorialized is American citizen Abdulrahman Al-Awlaki who was killed when an undisclosed branch of the United States government fired a missile into a restaurant in Yemen. At the age of 16, he was apparently the intended target of the attack. The only statement ever made by a US official explain- ing his murder was that he should have had a better father (Al- Awlaki was in Yemen searching for his father, also an Ameri- can citizen, who had been identified as an al Qaeda supporter, and assassinated in an American missile attack two weeks earlier).

Also included are Israeli Prime Minister Yitzak Rabin, murdered by a Jewish extremist for agreeing to make peace; Shannon Lowney, a 25-year old Planned Parenthood recep- tionist murdered at her desk by a Christian extremist; and, perhaps least well known, Rodney Dickens, who was eleven years old when he boarded American Airlines Flight 77 shortly before Islamic extremists crashed it into the Pentagon.

These events have all taken place within the last twenty years.

I HAVE shown above four key facts with which I now summarize in concluding this third and, I hope, final part of *The Age of Reason*:

1. The causes of science and human rights have progressed together, and in concert, since the end of the Christian Dark Ages, leading us to a new understanding of the natural world and the place of human beings in it. This progress has been against the continuing opposition of the churches, and remains under attack by fundamentalist Christians, Muslims and Jews who draw support from more moderate religious believers, and from their manipulation of governments.

2. All true systems of morality come from within the human race, and are measured by the respect shown to the rights and reason of human beings. It is only from a proper respect for these things that correct values can be established regarding the well-being of our planet and its other inhabitants, and the proper role of government and of commercial organizations in our society.

3. Believers in supernatural causes and powers continue to be manipulated by those who unjustly profit from, and rule over other human beings through that manipulation. The world will never be safe or free from this oppression until its people reject religious superstitions in all their forms, and cease in their teaching to impressionable and vulnerable children.

4. America's Founders were correct in seeking to protect the freedom and well-being of its people by erecting a wall of separation between church and state. This fundamental American principle is under attack by those who would use government to impose their religious beliefs upon others, and by foreign entities which use religious loyalties to manipulate American policy. It is our duty to resist these efforts and to advance freedom from religious interference in all our public affairs.

The implications of these facts are clear, and so, I believe it is incumbent upon all Americans - indeed upon all freedom loving peoples everywhere - to call an end to the dangerous and privileged position given to religious faith in modern society. This will require time, and must be carried out with equal respect for the rights of religious believers and those who have given up such beliefs. Following are the principal steps which I now conclude must be taken by all Americans, working together, who wish to promote a humane and enlightened world:

1. Ceasing, in ordinary social relations, to treat superstitions proclaimed on the basis of religious faith with the same respect that is due to facts established by evidence and reason;

2. Eliminating tax exemptions and other direct and indirect supports given by governments to churches and other religious organizations, including removal from all churches of the power of state agency in the sanctioning of marriage contracts;

3. Discouraging in all legal ways the teaching of supernatural beliefs to persons below the age of eighteen, and the compulsory inclusion of such persons in religious indoctrination and rituals, all of which practices should be considered abusive to the legitimate rights of children;

4. Denying all forms of political support or aid, with the exception of assistance in the genuine defense of human rights, to any country maintaining an official state religion, or which denies equal rights to any person on account of religious beliefs or the lack thereof;

and lastly, reclaiming our proper national motto:

E Pluribus Unum.

If Americans would but adopt a modern and reasoned attitude toward religious belief, denying it any place of favor in society and any influence whatever in the public affairs of our nation, they would cast a light into the darkest corners of the world and once again point the way to a future based on freedom and respect for the equal rights of all. It is my greatest hope that Americans will rise to this new challenge, and will at last bring our Age of Reason to its full and complete fruition.

ABOUT THE AUTHOR

Robert Shear has made an avocation of presenting to the public important characters from American history. He developed the Gerrit Smith Virtual Museum based on the unique collection of 19th century historical documents held at Syracuse University. On behalf of the National Park Service, he developed and the first full interpretive websites for the Women's Rights National Historical Park in Seneca Falls, New York and the Frederick Douglass National Historic Site in Anacostia, Virginia. He subsequently developed the popular repository of online history at NYHistory.com, hosting websites for the Harriet Tubman Home and the Central New York Freedom Trail Project, among many others.

His first solo venture in print, *Thomas Paine's The Age of Reason - Part Three* reflects three years of research into the history of science, religion and human rights, supplementing a career-long interest in these subjects. The book has earned praise for its style and scholarship both from Paine historians and from readers of popular literature.

Mr. Shear holds a Masters degree from the School of Public Health at Johns Hopkins University and completed his doctoral studies in Health Policy & Administration at the University of North Carolina at Chapel Hill. In his forty year career in public service he spent several years as an independent consultant and has held leadership positions in state government and several nonprofit organizations.

He currently resides in the high desert of the American Southwest.

Notes

1   *Essay on Dream*, which also contained a portion of Paine's previously published *An Examination of the Passages in the New Testament, quoted from the Old, and called Prophecies of the Coming of Jesus Christ*, was referred to by his biographer (Conway), but not by the author, as a continuation of The Age of Reason. - ed.

2   The will, dated January 1809 makes specific reference to a manuscript for Part Three, which would be senseless if the work had already been published. In *Origin of the Free-Masons*, published by Madame Bonneville after his death, Paine refers to previous chapters, believed to be among the lost portions of the original Part Three. -ed.

3   See Conway's Preface to *The Life of Thomas Paine* (Volume One), 1893, for a discussion of his efforts to locate Paine's lost papers. - ed.

4   Mr. Conway has shared his assumptions regarding my having discussed the six planets in the solar system when, as he points out, seven were known at the time the earlier Parts of this work were published. Based on this observation he has assumed that some or all of Part One was produced prior to 1781, the year in which the Herschels discovered the planet we now call Uranus. This is not the case. Mr. Conway flatters me with a greater attention to astronomy than I had maintained during the years of our Revolutionary War, and thereafter, and has assumed I brought with me on my departure from America more of my papers than were in fact in my possession. My instruction in the operations of our Solar System took place before I first left England, and for the most part after the transit of Venus observed in 1769. Thus, I was later able to calculate the approximate distances to the planets known at that time by recalled information and formula. In Part One I noted my attendance at demonstrations by Martin, which of course included his six-planet orrery. I have subsequently learned that I was already imprisoned in the Luxembourg by the time Jefferson, more the scientist than myself - and certainly of greater means - obtained from London the seven-planet orrery that remains today at Monticello.

Notes

5   *From Jesus to Constantine* by Bart D. Ehrman
    Origins of the Human Mind by Stephen P. Hinshaw
    Understanding the Secrets of Human Perception
        by Peter B.Vishton
    Einstein's Relativity and the Quantum Revolution
        by Richard Wolfson

6   In the earlier Parts of *The Age of Reason*, the author used
    the term *Bible* to refer to the Hebrew Bible, what
    Christians now call the Old Testament, and the term
    Testament for what is now called the New. In Part Three,
    the more common modern terminology is used. - ed.

7   After fleeing England to avoid arrest, the author was
    seated in the Convention called to write a new French
    Constitution as the delegate from Calais. - ed.

8   Following publication of Part Two, I became aware of the
    process by which I and my prison-mates were spared. As I
    explained in my letter to the National Intelligencer
    (December 29, 1802), when the executioner's mark was
    placed on the door to the room in which we were lodged, it
    happened the door was open flat against the wall, and the
    mark was made on the inside, thereby making it invisible
    to the passing jailer once the door was closed. Whether
    this was done as a result of accident or contrivance I
    cannot say.

9   Chapter XIV

10 I note here my own assumption that other worlds in our
    solar system were populated by humans has also been
    overthrown.

11 Among the authors whose works were also published by
    Joseph Johnson was the philosopher William Godwin.
    Mary Wollstonecraft met Mr. Godwin at an event
    sponsored by Mr. Johnson, at which I had the honor of
    making an address. While they did not get on especially
    well on that occasion, they later formed a strong bond, and
    gradually fell in love. Ms. Wollstonecraft died in
    childbirth, presenting to the world her namesake, the future
    bride of the English poet Percy Shelley. Shelley, it turned
    out, was a devotee of the work of Erasmus Darwin and
    shared with his wife an anecdote from Darwin about a

Notes

form of life discovered in the lead gutters of buildings in England which appeared to remain indefinitely inanimate when dehydrated, but which, when exposed to water, rapidly re-grew and displayed vigorous signs of life. Mary Wollstonecraft Shelley cited this anecdote in an introduction to her most famous work, as one of the ideas which inspired her cautionary tale of science gone wrong.

12 *The Botanic Garden*, 1791

13 At almost the same time I was warned by William Blake to leave England immediately lest I be arrested for arguing the Rights of Man, Joseph Priestly (who discovered the existence of oxygen, among other things) was similarly forced to flee, in his case to America, for daring to discuss openly the implications of his findings, and those of other natural philosophers. The mobs which destroyed Priestly's laboratory and scattered his books and papers painted on the walls "For King and Christ."

14 I also believed at that time, as was commonly the case, in the eternal divisibility of matter. It is now our understanding that indivisible quanta make up the basic structure of matter.

15 National Science Foundation Survey of Public Attitudes Toward and Understanding of Science and Technology. A survey experiment showed that 48% of respondents said they thought it was true that "human beings, as we know them today, developed from earlier species of animals," but 72% gave this response when the same statement was prefaced by "according to the theory of evolution." Similarly, 39% of respondents said that "the universe began with a huge explosion," but 60% gave this response when the statement was prefaced by "according to astronomers."

16 The international division of the Gallup Organization regularly compiles a Global Index of Religiosity and Atheism based on surveys of religious beliefs conducted throughout the world.

17 Part One, Chapter II

Notes

18 Such instruction will begin in the public schools of Ireland in fall of 2014

19 Christopher Hitchens offers this criticism in his chapter on *The Age of Reason* in his 2006 book *Thomas Paine's Rights of Man.*

20 As I noted in Part Two, the character of Satan appears in Job. Another reference in Zechariah is disputed. The word satan appears in some other passages, properly translated as *adversary*. The name Lucifer derives from the Latin word for Morning Star, an appellation directed by Isaiah to the then-current king of Babylon. The King James translators interpreted this as an alternate name for Satan, which it was not.

21 An AP/GfK Poll conducted in December 2011 showed 70% of surveyed American adults said they believed in angels.

22 Part One, Chapter XVII

23 It is not known if this John is the same as either the Evangelist or the Apostle, or if all three were different people.

24 *Angels*, 1975, 1986, 1994

25 Thomas Jefferson to Peter Carr, August 10, 1787

26 *Three Discourses on the Religion of Reason*, 1859

27 The actual number of practicing Mormons is disputed by some who claim the process of leaving is so burdensome that many simply abandon it, and continue to be counted by the church as active members.

28 For a discussion of the likely sources of the book's true origins, see Jockers, Witten and Criddle, *Reassessing Authorship of the Book of Mormon Using Delta and Nearest Shrunken Centroid Classification*, Literary and Linguistic Computing, December 2008; 23:465-491

29 In Part Two of this work I supposed that when Satan showed to Jesus "all the kingdoms" no notice was taken of America because it presumably had none. Here we are told one did exist, but apparently escaped notice nonetheless.

Notes

30 Prior to his claims about the Book of Mormon, Smith had offered his services for hire as a treasure hunter, in which he purported to be aided by means of crystal gazing. He was arrested for fraud in Pennsylvania, charged by a man who believed his uncle was being fleeced by Smith. The case was dismissed when the uncle testified on Smith's behalf.

31 Like other Christian churches Mormons reserve the Priesthood and all positions of authority within their church to men.

32 Here is another case, as I described in Part One, where the fraud, pious or not, is so intimately intertwined with the practices of the faith as to make the whole a farce.

33 The Book of Abraham is found in the Mormon publication titled *The Pearl of Great Price.*

34 For evidence of Joseph Smith's other spurious translations of actual and fabricated artifacts, the reader is referred to Grant H. Palmer's *An Insider's View of Mormon Origins*.

35 After he was exposed to the practices of Free-Masons, Smith adopted many of their symbols and temple rituals, likely unaware of the group's philosophical origins among sun-worshiping Druids.

36 For an introduction to the history and practices of the Church of Scientology, the reader is referred to a recent publication by Lawrence Wright entitled *Going Clear – Scientology: Hollywood & The Prison of Belief.*

37 According to its authors, *A Course in Miracles* was delivered by the voice of Jesus to the mind of New York psychologist Helen Schucman, who dictated what she heard to a colleague, reminiscent of the process used by Muhammad and possibly by Joseph Smith. It is perhaps interesting to note the last name of Schucman's collaborator was Thetford, the same as my place of birth.

38 An excellent example of this approach, combined with a quite sophisticated strategy for conditioning the reader to substitute subjective enthusiasm for objective evidence can be found in the book titled *E2* by Pam Grout. The first of the "scientific experiments" proposed in this book invites

the Universe, in effect, to prove the author's concepts by creating something totally unexpected in the reader's life sometime in a two week period. Criteria for success are not determined before the aspiring mystic spends two weeks looking for this sign. Events as unremarkable as a stranger sitting next to a person on a park bench are celebrated in the book as evidence of success. This is, of course, the very opposite of a Scientific Experiment, in which elaborate controls are put into place in advance of a test to protect against known *threats to validity,* which include the conscious and unconscious biases of the experimenter, and the natural tendency to seek an outcome consistent with experimenter expectations.

39   *Y*ouTube.com/watch?v=qsH1U7zSp7k

40 *Proof of Heaven*, 2012. This book is notable, if only for the author's remarkable success at incorporating into its pages a near-comprehensive catalog of popular New Age myths, fables and pseudo-scientific arguments.

41 As example, Michael Leavitt, who implemented President George W. Bush's Faith Based Initiative as Secretary of Health and Human Services, is currently giving speeches in which he argues the legitimacy of this position. He proposes to audiences in his speech on Religious Freedom that when laws are finally passed - as they inevitably will be - to protect members of the LGBT community from discrimination (such laws being necessary to reverse discriminatory legislation and State Constitutional amendments adopted at the behest of Leavitt's own church, among others) believers must assure they include special exemptions for those whose sensitivities are offended by such equality.

42   Matthew 6:5-6

43   *The Family: The Secret Fundamentalism at the Heart of American Power,* 2008, by Jeff Sharlett

44   April 2, 2014 Archbishop Emeritus Tutu Statement via Oryx Media

45 Diplomatic relations between the United States and the Catholic Pope ("The Holy See") were re-established in

Notes

1984 as part of the Cold War partnership between President Ronald R. Reagan and Pope John Paul II, 117 years after they were officially terminated by an act of Congress.

46 A March 2014 case in Louisiana (Scott and Sharon Lane v. Sabine Parish School Board) warrants mention, if only because it evidently reflects offenses more uncommon in the prosecution than in the commission. The case involves a child attending the sixth grade in public school where the teacher's lesson plan called for children to fill in in the blank in the sentence "ISN'T IT AMAZING WHAT THE ___ HAS MADE!!!!!!!!!!!!!!!!" The child, raised in a Buddhist home, failed to enter the expected reference to the Lord, and was denounced by the teacher in front of the class as stupid for not believing in God. When the child's parents complained to the local school superintendent, they were informed that in the "Bible Belt" they should expect the Christian God to be taught in schools, and if this was not accepted by them they would perhaps better take their child to a community where there were more Asians. The court ordered school district staff to undergo training in the religious rights of children, to be provided by the American Civil Liberties Union.

47 As of this writing the most recent data available from the federal government is from 2005, when the amount was estimated at $2.1 billion.

48 National Abortion Federation Statistical Report INCIDENTS OF VIOLENCE & DISRUPTION AGAINST ABORTION PROVIDERS IN THE U.S. & CANADA 1977-2012

49 "Mormons Tipped Scale in Ban on Gay Marriage" The New York Times, November 14, 2008